MW00914105

Dreams and Astrological Psychology

The Way through the
Maze of the Unconscious

John D. Grove

HopeWell
Knutsford, England

First published in the U.K. in 2014 by HopeWell

HopeWell
130 Grove Park, Knutsford
Cheshire WA16 8QD, U.K.

Edited by Barry Hopewell

ISBN 978-0-9558339-9-1

Dedicated to

This book is dedicated to my wife Judith B. Grove.

Acknowledgements

Thanks to Tommaso Nelli for the cover picture.

And acknowledgements to my tutor Trish Crawford, who has guided me in my studies in the Diploma Course of the Astrological Psychology Association.

About the Author

John D. Grove is recently retired from the Department of Veterans Affairs Hospital in Altoona, Pennsylvania where he had been employed as a clinical social worker for 29 years. He has been in private practice as a psychotherapist for 18 years and currently conducts therapy out of his home office. He lives with his wife, Judith B. Grove in Altoona, Pennslyvania.

Contents

vi

Preface

Sitting in a classroom at Elizabethtown College that spring in 1968, I was reporting on an assignment for the class in personality theory, based on the work of Carl Gustav Jung. What interested me the most was concepts like the Self, the Shadow and the Anima, which were beyond what I learned in the cognitive psychology which was being touted at the time. I had gone to college from a small town in central Pennsylvania where I changed my identity from a popular extravert who would take the homecoming queen to a football match to a studious, long-haired and introspective psychology major who wrote poetry.

In the field of literature I came across the author Herman Hesse, who was an analysand of Jung. Hesse wrote three books that influenced my thinking. The first was *Siddhartha*, about the life of Buddha, which was an assignment for summer reading in preparation for my freshman year. Enlightenment was achieved by conscious effort, transcending the ego and getting to the higher Self, a concept compatible with Jungian psychology.

The second book, *Demian,* explained the relativity of good and evil through two opposite types of character: Sinclair and Demian. Sinclair was the middle class, sheltered young man and Demian was the desire-filled, passionate protagonist who introduced Sinclair to the carnal tastes of the world. *Demian* changed my ideas about the Christian views of good and evil; as it embraced Abraxas, the god of good and evil.

The third book was *Steppenwolf.* Its main character, Henry Haller, was a misfit and recluse. He was in touch with his Shadow side which appealed to my more uncultured manners. At the close of his life Harry was addicted to alcohol yet understood the arcane and occult philosophies. He was well studied, but was a tragic and isolated man who felt like a wolf of the steppes.

I experimented with the traits of these three characters and took on some of their practices: yoga from *Siddhartha*, probing deeper into Jung's Shadow concept from *Demian*, and pursuing a lonely but single minded journey like Harry Haller in *Steppenwolf.*

Coming home to the small Pennsylvania town of Huntingdon after my senior year in college at the University of Ghana, I was aware that I wanted to delve further into the unconscious. I had studied African primal religion and the sociology of religion in Ghana and realized the link between sacred acts in religion and psychology.

Further, I witnessed firsthand the effect of "bad juju" on a colleague at the university whose 3 wives were in competition for his attentions; one of them enacted bad juju on him. When he came back, he lost 40 pounds and was weakened; he could no longer play tennis with me due to the psychological suggestion perpetrated on him by the village group-ego. This was an example of Anima possession on a tribal or collective level. I knew there were unseen forces at work behind the scenes that were transforming people without their willing participation.

In 1970, as I was reviewing the *Dell Astrology* magazine, I saw a boxed advertisement for 'Astroanalysis', a computer-generated character analysis based on date, time and place of birth. I sent in 5 dollars and got a report in 2 weeks. It hit me! I was a Sagittarius rising – now that meant travel, long journeys to foreign lands, philosophy, and interest in the higher mind. That did fit me pretty well and was akin to my soul's purpose at the time, I thought. There were 'darker' aspects in my horoscope that affected my emotions due to the alignment of the planets: Pluto and Venus led to my attraction to the hidden knowledge of the ages and oppositions between Neptune and the Moon accounted for my dreamy moods.

The Astroanalysis chart interpretation was written by a Teaneck, New Jersey astrologer named Charles Cook. His home was near Farleigh-Dickenson University in Rutherford, New Jersey where I went to get my Masters degree that fall of 1970. I was determined to meet the man. When I knocked on his door in spring of 1971, little did I know the influence he would have on my life. I bought the books he recommended: a table of houses, an ephemeris, and Alan Leo's *Astrology for All*. These were the tools I needed, along with Charles' worksheets and instruction, to cast horoscopes. I became his apprentice. I arranged to have Charles do interpretations of the graduate faculty at the School of Human Development at Farleigh-Dickenson University where I was enrolled for my Master's degree. That was a watershed moment for me – the faculty was impressed with his character analysis and I was determined to find out more about astrology.

In 1971, I was sitting cross-legged on the floor in a Long Island monastery for a graduate seminar on a Journaling Workshop. I was mesmerized by Dr. Ira Progoff who was teaching about the Jungian method of dream recording and interpretation. It was my first journal workshop from Progoff, who founded Dialogue House in New York City, but not my last. I learned how to record my dreams and to interpret them according to his methods. Dr. Progoff was a Jungian and I thought I was too. This started my journey into the healing profession of counseling and psychotherapy, which I have been practising for 40 years as a clinical social worker.

For all these years, I have considered myself practicing my craft based on Jungian theory. I have used the Psychology of Types to understand my patients and have completed dream interpretations and used active imagination with those who showed an aptitude for inner reflection.

All through my career, I kept up my astrological hobby for the insights it gave into the developmental issues of myself and my patients. This led me to Dr. Maureen Demot in 1997, who blended Jungian psychology with astrology. I took her course and received a diploma from her school of Astrological Psychology. But now as I end my career and am in early retirement, I feel torn between my life as an astrologer and my life as a mental health psychotherapist working in a hospital based setting. I have lived in two worlds, which became increasingly difficult to integrate: the empirical psychotherapy in my daily work versus consultations using astrological psychology.

Privately the usual justifications exist and I can prepare my defense. But astrological psychology cannot be brought out into the sun to be scrutinized by my professional colleagues. It is too vulnerable to be measured for efficacy by standards that are not suited to it. So I have to be cautious and preserve its precious caldron of meanings, insights and esoteric proclamations.

Today I have written this book to state my position and make it clear what I believe and why. Because I am in early retirement, I feel less threatened by being marginalized due to my beliefs and practices by a profession that does not endorse my values. So here is not my defense but the foundation of a new way of finding meaning in life in pursuit of being mentally healthy. I propose to make us all our own psychologists for it is possible for anyone inclined to reflection to try to understand the puzzle of their own psychic existence.

x

Introduction

This treatise is an attempt to provide explanation and direction to others. It provides a link between astrological psychology using the Huber method with my dream work over the years. The tools I have used to explain these come from exhaustive research into the nature of the psyche using the Jungian model. Superimposed on the Jungian understanding of the functioning psyche is the Age Progression of astrological psychology, along with transits that coincide with developmental challenges throughout my life. This is a self study and longitudinal.

I think the approach I use here may appear too subjective for some but it is unique and provides a perspective in self analysis that may prove useful to those disciplined students and serious searchers for the appearance of a spark of the divine in our lives. There is today a movement to change current paradigms of understanding of the psyche to be more comprehensive and less materialistic. I am happy to be a part of this movement. I put forth this work as a testament to my predecessors: C.G. Jung, Bruno and Louise Huber and the many researchers who paved the way for this new psychology to be manifested.

I. The Prevailing Waning Consciousness

The conscious psyche in the life of people is the focus of mental health treatment, especially as it relates to individuals in the constantly shifting and changing world of the 21st century. The Western development of therapeutic treatments to heal the imbalance of psychic troubles has been in existence only since the early 1800's and only systematically studied since the 1900's. The 20th century saw the emergence of *The Diagnostic and Statistical Manual of Psychiatric Disorders*, which is a compendium of atheoretical behaviors, in which patients have clusters of symptoms which they bring to consulting rooms of mental health professionals. With the advent of effective psychotropic medications in the 1960's many people who were institutionalized could be discharged because the medications they were given controlled their symptoms with reduced side effects, allowing them to live somewhat independently.

These two developments: a classification system of mental disorders and psychotropic medication have shaped the field of psychotherapy in the Western world, but not for the best. Diagnostic categories pigeonhole and label people in a calibrated manner. Medications lessen delusions and hallucinations, thus creating classes of professionals who are technicians to analyze symptoms and their meaning (psychologists) or reduce symptoms (psychiatrists) – thus minimizing important personal content and context that could aid in solving the patients' problems. This treatment focus may reduce symptoms but does not provide insight into the genesis of the problem – or take into consideration the personal unconscious. Thus we have settled for a mediocre standard of mental health care, rather than being focused on healing patients by helping them find meaning in their lives so that they could be better integrated, balanced human beings.

Western societies define psycho-pathologies of their people in relation to the degree of negative adaptation to their societies. These maladaptive behaviors are assessed by identifying the lack of functional survival skills. Positive survival skills are those that have high value in capitalistic societies: ability to hold a job, to have healthy partner relationships and be able to distinguish between what is real and what is fantasy. Although these are desirable traits to have for the general population, there is an underclass of people that cannot perform in a complex society. Through identification of individuals as permanently mentally disabled, we are forcing conformity on the patient based on dominant and relative social and cultural values. These value-based assumptions of what in society constitutes healthy occupational, relationship and reality testing adjustment is used much too literally to determine eligibility for pensions and services in our capitalistic system. The trend was apparent in the mental health assessments, where compensation judges weighed the evidence of disability on the basis of too many factors that were too literal and permanently stigmatizing; this was due to the narrowness of our cultural definitions of what are acceptable behaviors and healthy adaptation. Due to this our numbers of underclass citizens is growing. Furthermore, these cultural definitions of what constitutes 'normal behavior' do not fit with the demographic changes that will occur by 2050, when there will be more Hispanic and Asian populations with different personality traits based on their cultural values.

Examples of this prejudice toward the mentally ill are society created diagnostic categories: obsessive compulsive and dependent personality disorders. (Source *Diagnostic and Statistical Manual of the American Psychiatric Association* – 5). Dependent personality disorders are the target of welfare reform politicians who think people are too lazy to work.

Diagnostic Statistical Manual V (DSM-V) has eliminated the category of personality disorders from its diagnostic categories and that is an improvement. The labels of personality disorders are traits that are developmentally transitory. They can be cured – for example, research shows dialectic behavioral therapy improves symptoms of borderline personality disorder. Historically, these labels shut out people from job opportunities. If one had a medical discharge or other than honorable discharge from the military due to a personality disorder, that label closed doors and shut out job opportunities. If one has traits of perfectionism, over concentration on details, checking and re-checking one's work, spending long hours working, not being able to see the big picture, and having obsessive thoughts that interfere with functioning off the job – that is a desirable employee. Yet these obsessive compulsive traits, when they are a personality disorder are grounds for dismissal when they effect productivity and quotas in the workplace. I have personally seen people fired for this diagnosis who are overburdened in making quotas for performance in documentation.

In addition, those who develop a dependence on others for support, have difficulty with decision making, need others to assume responsibility for major areas of life, and are unrealistically preoccupied with fears of being left to care for themselves are those who have a dependent personality disorder. (DSM-V) These traits also may be time-limited and situational, but the label remains. So we have created institutions and adjudication patterns that perpetuate disability and dysfunction based on criteria that may not be relevant now or in the future. By assessment alone and not mandating treatment, we perpetuate these disorders rather than heal them; plus we stigmatize a whole class of people.

So we have created institutions that perpetuate disability and dysfunction, based on criteria that may not be relevant now or in the future. By assessment alone and not treatment, we perpetuate these disorders rather than heal them.

For centuries Western societies have framed the cultural definition of mental health. The universal acceptance of English as the language of science has created the psychological norms as to what constitutes healthy individual adaptation. Further, the ability of United States and Western Europe to dominate, with English spoken as the key to business institutions, has enabled us to define the economic *zeitgeist* or 'spirit of the times'. This has amounted to a monopoly on banking and global markets.[1] But now that is breaking down, as the recent dominance of Western societies is being challenged the world over.

We shall now evaluate on individual and collective levels what have been the prevailing sociological trends that have captivated both psychological man and his economics since the Enlightenment. And we shall point out how they are breaking down in the face of the equalizing effect of globalization and the universal internet. We are searching for an answer to the dilemma facing modern man and need to take him out of the illusion that the ego is the center of the psyche; the answer is more comprehensive than the narrow view propagated by academic psychology and economics.

When we survey Western models of treatment of the pathological psyche, the academic and treatment focus is concentrated on building ego strengths. The assertions and conclusions that are research based are backed up by empirical studies. Accordingly, psychotherapies emphasize statistically relevant truths. They are called 'evidenced based psychotherapies'.

Most psychotherapies are designed to build a healthy 'executive function' of the ego through cognitive strategies.[2] Healthy ego functioning is perceived by mental health professionals as the focus of treatment. The norm is treating maladaptive behaviors that are the result of poor ego development, such as confused ego identity, low ego esteem and unhealthy defense mechanisms. This is appropriate for ego development in youth and early adulthood. But this treatment focus on ego building falls short when it is applied to the whole life cycle. The underlying assumption is fallacious, because the ego strength that is important to survival at the youth and young adult stages of the life cycle is increasingly maladaptive in mid-life and beyond.

How adaptive would it be for a 40 year old man to start an identity search for the first time? Although mid-life crises at this age create the desire to find a new identity, isn't it based more on existential searches for meaning, rather than just finding a new wife or occupational niche? For a woman aged 65, is it adaptive for her to concentrate on her health concerns to lengthen her life and beauty to the exclusion of finding the meaning and purpose of those culturally defined symptoms?

I propose that this cognitive ego based intervention model is unsound for the healthy psyche, putting too much emphasis on youth without including the rest of the life cycle – especially when ego energies wane and spiritual energies wax, as in later life. The approach of current ego psychology ignores the symptoms of psychic disturbances due to crises of a spiritual nature – on which it is silent and ignorant.[3]

The value system of this Western psychological treatment approach supports the beliefs that individualism is the end-all and purpose of man in society. This view is supported by the clichés that 'time is money' and one has to develop his/her ego potential and dominate over others or else lose to competitors, 'you have to take your chances, you may not get another one' and to be successful one has to possess the conscious attitude of the all-important and 'youthful' approach to life.

These views as applied on the world stage imply metaphorically that capitalistic, imperial dominance of one country over another, usually through military means, is the answer in the global competition for limited commodities and resources. This view is an anachronism based on Social Darwinism. To perceive that one nation state can dominate others – exploit them – is no longer pragmatic in a global society where the rights of sovereign states are supported by international law and the United Nations. To survive today, we must learn global cooperation or else we shall extinguish our existence by war, famine and disease thus ending humanity as we know it on earth.

When the ego fails to serve our survival needs, when chaotic losses enter into our lives, the ego breaks down – and all the support which that psychic structure has given us fails. Futile attempts to find reasons why bad events happen to us fill the case notes of many psychotherapists. The suffering ego may cause us to avenge those who are the 'reasoned' sources of our pain. We have borne witness to the attacks on Afghanistan and then Iraq by former President Bush's administration in retaliation for 9/11.

But that outmoded path only perpetuates conflict. Profound self-examination is called for by our leaders and individuals in our society. For that to happen, psychological insight into our spiritual roots is needed so that assertive, not aggressive interventions may do for nation states instead of hurting our people and our sovereignty. Thus a spiritual journey awaits us and our leaders – and humility is called for, not ego-bound self righteousness. Reflecting on observing ourselves and learning to be receptive to intuitive guidance is the answer – even when doing so may humiliate us and defy reason.[4] This can go a long way to creating a new world view to support the survival of humanity. But these changes need to occur on both a national and an individual level to be fully implemented. Carl Gustav Jung in his last work *The Undiscovered Self*, points to the problem:

> "Our (collective) psyche is profoundly disturbed by the loss of moral and spiritual values that have kept our life in order. Our consciousness is no longer capable of integrating the natural afflux of concomitant, instinctive events that sustains our conscious psychic activity. This process can no longer take place in the same way as before, because our consciousness has deprived itself of the organs by which the auxiliary contributions of the instincts and the unconscious could be assimilated. The organs were the numinous symbols, held holy by common consent."[5]

Historically, conscious spatial perceptions in the West were structured according to guarding and protecting land and property rights. This had psychological implications creating vigilance and mistrust toward our competitors. We still have the view that land we bought with money is our possession. And thus we develop a collective defensive attitude based on protectionism, exploitation of resources and imperial power. In the last Iraq war, these assumptions came to light as we intruded on a sovereign country to kill a terrorist regime, to democratize them and to prevent the expansion of their nuclear capability. On a large level 'manifest destiny' is just a global form of egocentric narcissism. And the underlying, covert rationale for these actions was the motive of taking resources that did not belong to us.

Another example, on a national level, is the American business practice of the cement curbing off stores along a strip of highway, to protect access. This possessive protection of land out of self-interest and for money is ingrained in our citizens and our culture. Of course, this makes it hard on the consumer who may want to compare prices of competing businesses and makes him/her labor for that opportunity.

Add to this the rights of property owners to defend themselves against perceived intruders by 'the gun'. It is now a law that if someone enters your property without just cause, you can shoot him or her. This has led to tragic results – even fathers killing their own sons. It highlights the hypocrisy with which we conduct ourselves internationally and at home.

Today's American ethos and myth that more education leads to upward social mobility promises more than it can deliver. Job markets are based on the principles of supply and demand, scarcity and competition. The fact is that this social advancement is open to only a few; as a driving motive for young adults, it cannot be sustained in the global market place. What has happened is that jobs for Americans do not just occur within our national boundaries but all over the world. More and more occupations require second languages and a view that we must have a global view if we are to survive in today's economic climate.

Overemphasis on the development of the individual conscious ego is valued over development of society, with the assumption that all are given equal opportunity to survive and fulfill themselves materially. Supporting this egocentric mind warp is the myth that there is a 'top-down', trickle-down economic benefit to the lower classes from the sterling enterprise of the wealthiest among us. Thus, we should be grateful that the wealthy create jobs for the rest of us. As stewards of this popular political illusion, the wealthy, we are told see people who are poor as lazy. It is only they with their positive motivation and enterprising spirit as capitalists who are the virtuous ones.

These views are "democratized" in a preferentially pluralistic society where only the wealthy can get access to lobbies that promote legislation that support and sustain their views of the world. The political result, for example, is to cut medical access and food stamps to the poor and to cut budgets for education for the young, rather than tax the wealthy. Head start programs for children and subsidies to universities are cut before raising taxes.

The paradox is that the higher one goes in the stratum of society in career advancement, the more one is able to violate the ego boundaries of others and dominate them, through the exercise of sex and power. For example, wealthy politicians, actors/actresses and sports stars are known for multiple sexual liaisons and not conforming to the boundaries of monogamy which is the norm in common society.

The computer has for decades replaced human workers on the job through automation. And more than that, statistics have become the language to justify, measure goals and award pay for good work performance. Now people in the work force are evaluated on how much they conform to performance measures, thresholds of achievement and productivity standards. Because this is often the only measure of work performance, it has dehumanized the process of workplace trust among people and created a lack of social responsibility. This one-sided way of measuring human achievement creates an imbalance in the individual and society leading to more dissatisfaction and mental illness in the workplace and society as a whole. This is due to the way the ego has dominated consciousness in the Western world; it has become inflated, as societies have become increasingly narcissistic – and devaluing of humanistic values and institutions becomes the norm.

Thus, the dominant values that this collective consciousness represents on a social-national-political level is reflected in the attitudes of individuals on a personal level as well. Both levels are reaching a critical point.

We now turn to new developments in our understanding of consciousness that transform individual and national perceptions of mental health, and our view of the way we conduct business in a global marketplace. The emergence of these new forms of consciousness has been accelerated by the internet, which equalizes the playing field for all people, as long as they have access to information. It changes the individual's perception and attitudes toward their world.

Thus, the evaluation of psychological and economic consequences of our ego-centric world view leads us nowhere except to our own destruction. The answer is self knowledge, not ego knowledge:

> *"if we had self knowledge that would not be the case (of "isms" dominating the world stage with terror). We stand face to face with the terrible question of evil and do not even know what is before us, let alone what to pit against it. And even if we did know, we still could not understand 'how it could happen here'. With glorious naiveté a statesman comes out with a proud declaration that he has no imagination for evil… we have not imagination for evil but evil has us in its grip… That is the psychological situation in the world today: some call themselves Christian and imagine that they can trample so-called evil underfoot by merely willing to; others have succumbed to it and no longer see the good. Evil today has become a visible Great Power. One half of humanity battens and grows strong on a doctrine fabricated by human ratiocination; the other half sicken from the lack of a myth commensurate with the situation."*[6]

II. The New Consciousness

We are on the cusp of a paradigm shift, some call it a new Age of Aquarius where deterministic values are becoming subservient to a more holistic approach that takes into account measurable, objective realities plus humanistic considerations such as the value of self-knowledge. As humanistic values seem to threaten the hold on materialistic and measurable approaches to truth, anxiety increases among the stewards of the old order. W. I. Thompson describes the phenomenon of "the sunset effect" that occurs at the end of a millennium, when the tenacity to hold onto waning values becomes more desperate as we move closer to the future with new values emerging.[7] Within the collective consciousness of the culture, there is a powerful tendency to see life through a rear view mirror and hold on to old worn-out values in the face of threatening changing times. Myths that reflect the *weltanschauung* and mesmerize our people into glorifying the times gone by are – 'The Fountain of Youth', 'The Spirit of Capitalism', the 'Magic Bullet', 'God and Country' and 'The Cowboy', to name but a few.

The propaganda proposed by reactionary politicians and established academic proponents of the status quo is using our fear of change to prevent us from realizing that the *"reality we are living in (which) remains largely unconscious, but (which) we acknowledge by grabbing back onto the sentimental things of the past"*[8] is gone forever.

Consciousness is becoming less bound by fear of poverty and pride in material wealth and more focused on the courage to be.[9] What this present reality means to the individual is that he/she can let him/herself be led by personal dreams to prepare for critical periods in life. But this is really a new process because it is possible only by a loss of old ego identifications. This is such a new awareness, to be able to stop our striving and look at subtle images, revealed by our personal visions. But it is also much more. It is also gaining a perspective on self-knowledge that involves personal timing of events in our lives as revealed by astrology. I use the Huber Method of astrological psychology.[10] But there are many valid psychological astrological approaches to discovery of one's true self.

Time, space and cause-and-effect explained the traditional approaches to empirically based psychotherapeutic truths, but a fourth concept introduces a significant and individualistic understanding to the behavior of humans, namely acausality. C.G. Jung discovered a synchronistic, connecting principle which asserted that meaningful coincidences existed between individual traits of character and astronomical data.

In his astrological experiment Jung look at 180 married couples with 50 solar-lunar aspects; he compared the 180 men with any one of the 180 women they were not married to. The results showed that in three *"fortuitously assorted batches of marriage horoscopes the greatest frequency fell to three different lunar conjunctions as follows: Moon in one conjunct Sun in the other; Moon conjunct Moon; Moon conjunct Ascendant."*[11a] Such correspondences between an individual's birth time and/or a given situation (marriage choices) was significant in giving astrology credibility as the probability that the results were due to chance was 1 in 2.5 million.

Jung believed, as does this writer, that the principle of synchronicity represents irrefutable and verifiable facts which go beyond empiricism. Synchronicity attunes us to meaningful psychic correspondences and goes beyond what is accepted in prevailing empirically based psychotherapy. And this present work assumes that synchronistic phenomena underlie the truths asserted here because of its relevance to meaningful psychic individual experience as exemplified in dreams, personality traits or other significant life events.[11b]

In the use of astrology here, we do not naively assert that planets *cause* behavior, but their aspects to each other, as reflected in the birth chart, are a reflection of psychological states and/or events explained by the principle of synchronicity. The ancient adage from the Library of Alexandria, 'as above, so below' fits very well into this way of thinking. Everything in the universe follows analogy; that which is truth on a macrocosm is repeated truth on the microcosm.

In *The Archetypal Cosmos*, Keiron Le Grice relates this with morphic fields discovered by Rupert Sheldrake and the persistence of the birth pattern as a reflection of formative causation.[12] He explains that, according to Sheldrake, information (like astrological aspects) can be transmitted to organisms and help to maintain their structure, as well as guide their actualization. Further, the birth pattern (horoscope) as a reflection of this type of information is evidence of a stratified order of nature. At this point, the implications point to a theoretical understanding and synthesis of a new paradigm of science that is still in its infancy. But these theories will certainly be validated in the future and they explain the truth behind astrology.

Dreams have been relegated to a small corner of psychological reality for individuals in our study of the psyche within the framework of ego psychology. But dreams are important to self-knowledge as they contain vital personal information and insights that can guide our inner and outer goals as we come up against the timing of events.

Esoteric astrology studies the primal causes and the underlying reality of our presumptive world. Developmental timing of opportunities to identify with the real Self rather than the false or inauthentic selves is akin to striving for that eternal calm beyond space and time dimensions, rather than doggedly striving for goal actualization in the outer world come 'hell or high water'.

Astrological psychology identifies timing of psychological effects that correspond with an 'Age Point' as it travels through the 12 houses of the horoscope at the rate of 6 years per house. It takes 72 years for the Age Point to go full cycle. Thus, there are times, determined by the placement of the Age Point, when it may be appropriate to charge ahead and times when it may be better to look inward. When the Age Point travels through the low point of a house, the individual may find this an appropriate time for reflection and looking inward. When the Age Point reaches the cusp of a house, there is more likely potential for accelerated activity. Throughout life the Age Point progresses through the houses which represent contexts for outer world activity; e.g. the 10th house represents individuality expression in the outer world or profession and the 4th house represents the sense of belonging to the collective or family. There are cusps and low points in each house and a corresponding cycle of inner and outer psychological orientation.

"Of the techniques used in Astrological Psychology, Age Progression – using the chart as a Life Clock – is often the one which most captures the imagination and interest. Age Progression is the Huber method of timing in the horoscope... The four Cardinal points – the Ascendant, the Descendant, the IC or cusp of the 4th house, and the Midheaven – are high energy areas of the high energy curve... there is a huge surge of energy at each of these four points, like a thrust or push out into the environment and the outside world... In time after this the energy falls off and is at its lowest at the Low Point, approximately two-thirds of the way through each house..."[13]

As the Age Point progresses, we learn to appreciate events in our lives in terms associated with the environmental domains of the houses.

"The astrological houses represent real and tangible life situations and areas of their detailed experience and activity... The configuration reference of one's house system will be stamped into behavioral traits through the upbringing in the personal environment."[14]

As the Age Point moves through the houses, intra-psychic activity can occur which conjures up images from the subconscious or super-conscious which manifest as dreams. When dreams are interpreted in conjunction with the timing of Age Point aspects, they can help re-orient the individual back to the Self, symbolic of that empty circle in the center of the horoscope. The empty point in the horoscope or central core *"symbolizes the soul, the spirit and the doorway to universal energy... connected to our Higher Self, or god; or it is a place where we connect to transpersonal energy."*[15]

Age Point aspects (angular relationships between two points) in the horoscope mark potentially critical periods in the developmental understanding of ego attachments. When the aspects are used with the dreams of that time, the dream interpretations can help to understand ego losses by helping the native to understand the context in the larger meaning of the life cycle. These interpretations can yield important psychological insights about when to act and when to retreat in the external world.

Jung explains, in the context of the function of religious symbols, that often the experience of the archetypes of God is channeled through in dreams:

> *"It was not the man Jesus who created the myth of the God-man; it had existed many centuries before. He himself was seized by this symbolic idea, which, as St. Mark tells us, lifted him out of the carpenter's shop and the mental narrowness of his surroundings. Myths go back to primitive story tellers and their dreams... (Civilized man) is blind to the fact that, with all his rationality and efficiency, he is possessed by powers beyond his control. The gods and demons have not disappeared at all, they have merely got new names. They keep him on the run with restlessness, vague apprehensions, psychological complications, an invincible need for pills, alcohol, tobacco, dietary and other hygienic systems..."*[16]

I believe that dreams are the language of God channeled through our Self and we ought to listen to and interpret them. At certain times, to hold back, to withdraw and retreat by introspectively reframing losses in external affairs is the mix that could help us to negotiate through the world of today. However, few Westerners can achieve the emotional detachment to persevere with studied reflection when potential losses occur in failure to achieve strategic life goals, such as loss of occupational identity, loss of role identity in the family or loss of bodily identity through illnesses that threaten ego integrity. But dreams that occur at these critical times, that indicate a reversal and change from a dominant ego identity to a submissive ego identity, could give us insights into different tactics of engagement with the external realities facing us. The application of ego detachments to our lives are blessings and curses, but they can be clues to dealing with loss.

Getting rid of the illusion that the ego is the seat of consciousness is most difficult without a road map. But being able to understand one's dreams, put them in the context of critical periods astrologically, and finally relinquish the ego attachment that allowed one to believe in the ego's dominance in the first place, can be a source of fulfillment and renewal.

Most Westerners face crisis or depression when facing such losses in occupation, relationships or their hold on reality. And the more they attempt to hold onto the ego identity that is threatened, and blame external factors for an internal process, the more mentally unbalanced they become. We Westerners are psychically one-sided with amalgamation of the ego identity to the persona or dominant function of our psychological type[17] and conscious identity. We attach our ego to our social face (persona), which we present to the world, and the role we play in society. Most of us take this role so seriously that we think that is our real identity and are loath to give it up. Once that persona is lost, our egos can be devastated and buckle under – collapsing like a house of cards.

We do not have the broad based foundation of wholeness with which to withstand losses when our dominant ego function is thwarted. This is because we know little of our personal inner processes and how our own personal and collective unconscious can interpret for us through dream imagery how to apply ourselves to real life events. Plus, we do not know alternative rituals to help us cope with the ego loss, in order to still feel psychologically secure. So this is the challenge that this work will try to address: helping people at critical times to relinquish the ego illusion as a dominant focus. Thus, we can find the true meaning of what is mentally healthy and balanced. Facing moral conflicts such as sin also applies here. Given that the sin of pride has everything to do with ego attachments, we will discuss temptation and the moral strength it takes to wrestle with desire. Desire to gain money, sexual pleasure, and avenge our enemies can occupy our minds and distract us from our communion with the Self. Meditation on mantras, rituals such as yoga or reciting spiritual verses daily are ways to find peace and keep centered around the Self rather than be bound by the ego and its desires. To keep focused on the Self requires humility.

Flexibility in psychic attitudes is called for, but not the ego's total annihilation. This shift is needed on both individual and collective levels. W. I. Thompson suggests that the emerging world is that of an integrated planetary consciousness in which all the old forms of industrial might – defense, territorial imperialism, and the work ethic – break down. In his article in *New Story*, he characterizes the new era:

"In the emerging planetary world, what counts can't be counted and so you don't have a world of objects that are separated in space – wealth and mansions here and dioxin dumps over there. You have a world of interpenetrating presences; you have a world in which consciousness is immanent in matter in that matter isn't separate from consciousness. You have a world of play, of performance, of a willingness to lower your lifestyle if that will increase the joy, and the spontaneity, and the innovation and the risk-taking, and the imaginative fun of being."[18]

On a national level, paralleled to the individual loss of ego identity, one can assume that with these dramatic shifts of collective power in governments, the change to being a second- or third-rate nation, or not being dominant as a world power, will be felt as having devastating effects on both the nation state and the individuals experiencing this loss.

How shall we endure such a shift of consciousness on so many levels without losing our psychological security? With the advent of self-psychology, mostly propagated by Carl G. Jung and the Jungians, comes the small but vigorous movement to re-define the nature of the psyche – rather than just focus on the narrow conscious mind of the behaviorists and ego psychology. Coming from its roots in Hinduism, the bible and ancient alchemy, the Self is seen as the center of the psyche, not the ego. And it is mostly unconscious.

"The recognition of this civilizational unconscious, this hidden cultural reality, is the end of a process that began intellectually in the early 20th century. Freud began with the instinctive unconscious. Jung followed him and reflected the instinctive life into consciousness as it was created in the collective unconscious and reflected in patterns of imagery that would occur in science or poetry or dreams or the rest of it. It wasn't instinct. It was instinct reflected in imagery creating consciousness."[19]

These images are filtered through the structure of the Self at the center of the psyche, which includes conscious and unconscious parts. Dreams come in images and enlighten the ego via the Self. What better focus for being centered on the Self than through the imagery of dreams?

III. Exploring the Wider Circumference of the Self

Individuation or movement toward wholeness of the psyche, with the effort to balance opposites within us being the goal of psychological man, is a more holistic goal than the support of egoism and 'winning at all costs' which is common to Western values.[20] This view offers the opportunity to learn to shift the major purpose of our lives from the ascendancy of the individual ego to a focus on identification with the Self. This reorientation tasks us to achieve a comprehensive reconciliation of the opposites and conflicts within us. To do this we must not shirk from the recognition of our battle with sin, both personal and collective. Through self-reflection we can achieve a balance in these forces, which through the ego threaten to divide our souls. This approach is particularly appropriate for middle age and beyond. And it never ends, but is fed by new material from the unconscious as we live on. In these ways we are looking forward to a new *Weltanschauung* or world view.

The qualitative, subjective information of our unconscious plays an equal part along with objective reality in reaching reconciliation of the opposites/conflicts within us on which our psychic balance depends.

James Hillman comments on this need for the inner searching needed to become authentic individuals in the following:

> *"When we do not listen to the subjective inner voice but depend instead only on objective reality as if we can control what is objective, we have committed an error. For we need to take co-responsibility for the world we elicit and enact thorough the creative power of interpretive strategies… as we grow and participate in finding truth."* [21]

Both the subjective and objective approaches to truth are valid. Therefore, there is equal emphasis on the inner, subjective man and on objective reality with its ego strengths as manifested in external goals. Dreams, the personal unconscious with its complexes, and the collective unconscious all play an important role in determining the holistic expression of the individual and balancing his psychic system. Instead of just seeking salvation outside ourselves, we are tasked to look within for our own blind-spots, sins, and shadowy parts of ourselves.

As a mental health professional knows, there are tradeoffs that a person makes in 'getting ahead' as he becomes aware of the cost to the balance of his psychic system, when he becomes too driven by external goals and too obsessed by them. A psychic one-sidedness develops; he has many blind spots – living a false self (or subpersonalities) only identifying with his/her social identity (persona), and buying into a competitive struggle for survival following what the ego wants.[22] But in order to achieve a healthy lifestyle, he tries to lessen stressors in his life to achieve the balance necessary to be a whole person or natural man.[23]

So the ego driven world is waning and in the works of Johnathon Zap, the ego may now in its present form at least, have exceeded its evolutionary purpose and be a type of psychic structure that is due for extinction/metamorphosis.[24]

When she re-orients herself toward the Self rather than the ego, the timing of events is perceived from a subjective dimension not just a fact-based, objective reality. Consider pre-cognitive dreams that are successfully interpreted and how time is broken down by their forecasting ability in predicting events. When the Self is perceived as generating conscious decisions, rather than consciousness creating self-direction, one is able to act on synchronistic insights that are simultaneous and telepathic. But the conscious ego with its willfulness is only prepared to dominate – and is the prevailing complex that motivates most people in the Western world. It will not die an easy death as a psychic structure. The obsessive, dark side of the ego, which sees itself as "God and as apart from the rest of the universe..." is driven by a will to bring external objects, animate and inanimate, under its control.[25] This pathologized version of the ego doesn't see itself as part of a living matrix, but rather looks out at an abstracted chessboard consisting of real estate, technology, (human flesh) and livestock waiting to be exploited."[26] And this is, in fact, how current political regimes and capitalistic, ego-driven persons in society see the world.

On a collective level, as old regimes fall and collective ego identities of nations change, it can be threatening to see the old order die and wait until a new order establishes itself. Witness the anxiety caused by the ubiquitous mass movements (like the Arab spring), which encompasses a change in hierarchies that have traditionally been part of countries' geopolitical identity. People all over the Arab world were moved to bring down their leaders and it was accomplished in simultaneous fashion; the masses were using electronic communication via computers, cell phones and ipads to organize mobs, protests and revolutions. During the Arab Spring, the masses desired to change the social order instead of trusting the isolated old order to usher in change. The ruling party in Egypt, for example, said these changes were evil because they threatened the survival of the state. But the Self which motivated the masses' collective consciousness to embrace action for freedom offered a broader perspective. (It is notable that there is an ongoing square aspect between Uranus in Aries, which represents revolutions and new beginnings, and Pluto in Capricorn, which represents renewal of government).

The masses were aware that a broken country is better than a corrupt one; there was awareness that good and bad were necessary for renewal and death of the old ego-driven world. So the Arab Spring movement came from the depths of the collective Self of the people and was not bound by fears of survival based on ego-security. As Jung would see it, the collective unconscious in this movement worked through the masses motivated by the collective Self.

"The Self (moreover) is an archetype that inviolably expresses a situation within which the ego is contained. Therefore, like every archetype, the Self cannot be localized in an individual ego-consciousness, but acts like a circumambient atmosphere to which no definite limits can be set, either in space or in time. (Hence the synchronistic phenomena so often associated with activated archetypes.)"[27]

As the world becomes more global and electronic media obliterates distance among geographical boundaries, making information accessible to all, we live in a discontinuous world where we are affected by events across the oceans and respond as if the events were in our town or own back yard.[28] This change breaks down traditional political hierarchies by spreading out information and authority to the personal level. It creates confusion for proponents of the status quo by creating universal awareness of cultural relativity. The church's priests, the role of doctors as supreme authority figures, and the paternalistic political systems become institutions that need to be ethically connected and include the common man as an equal and as a participant to be relevant. In this process, the individual is the authority and personal vision is the right vision.

James Hillman states in his *Healing Fiction* treatise, the kind of healing needed for modern man and woman is the *"blending of opposites; a male/female; objective/subjective; strong/weak; up/down sizing."*[29] This is a rather fictitious, unreal journey of experience if one lives it entirely. It is *"preposterous, unrealizable, non-literal, from which singleness of meaning is organically banned. Is this not fiction, per se? Is that why psychotherapy in desperation after centuries of enlightenment turned to myths to find support for its therapy?"*[30] This process of becoming whole again, advocating being a living paradox of opposites by "following your bliss" bespeaks of recognizing the need for unity and simplification.

To accomplish this, a spiritual motive is awakened and we highlight Ignatius Loyola's foundation for guidance as paraphrased by C.G. Jung:

> *"Man's consciousness was created to the end that it may (1) recognize its descent from a higher unity; (2) pay due and careful regard to this source; (3) execute its commands intelligently and responsibly; and (4) thereby afford the psyche as a whole the optimum degree of life and development."*[31]

Thompson explains:

> *"Individuality created a new dimension for consciousness to explore in the wider circumference of Self. But more, the process of individuation can be recognized as a kind of "circling the spiral" or Jung's mandala, eventually turning back towards the center."*[32]

The Huber Method of astrological psychology frees the energy to transcend the ego by proposing an identification with the Self as the individual is guided by a developmental-spiritual journey.[33] There are five levels in this system. The first level is the conditioning from the environment which effects behavior on a most superficial level of consciousness (the houses). The second is the influence of the signs of the zodiac (Aires, Taurus, Gemini, etc) representing inherited qualities of consciousness. The third is the planets which influence the psychological drives and states of awareness. The fourth is the aspects and patterns of geometric figures which influence unconscious motivation and perception. The fifth is the central core of the circle which represents the Self or inner being which is an awareness beyond all conditioning, forces of personality or inheritance. See Figure 1.

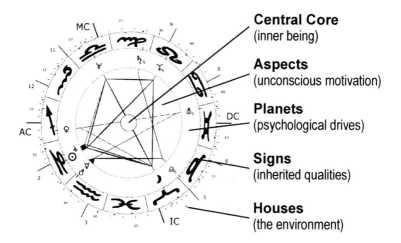

Central Core
(inner being)

Aspects
(unconscious motivation)

Planets
(psychological drives)

Signs
(inherited qualities)

Houses
(the environment)

**Figure 1. The Five Levels
shown in the Author's Natal Chart**

Aspect patterns provide the hint to one's unconscious motivation and dominant ego-identifications that are budding in young adulthood, into mid-life but waning with the more introspective focus of later years. An aspect of ego attachment – the occupational identity is not easy to give up. Witness many elders unable to quit their jobs at retirement age because their lives would be empty. Without their occupational identity and persona, they are 'nothing'.

However, loss of occupational identity can be the beginning of a different kind of journey and not an end. It is a process not reserved for retirement alone. The process takes years of psychological preparation and can lead to a rebirth experience. In the Huber Method of astrological psychology every 72 years marks a complete Age Point cycle. Psycho-physical development starts at birth. The Age Point journeys around the circle of the 12 houses, each one representing an area of environmental influence on the individual. The 360-degree circle ends with the return of the Age Point to the ascendant, the point where it began. (See Figure 2).

As the Age Point prepares a return to the ascendant lessons learned by outer experiences can enrich the soul spiritually. At these stages of life, the cycle returns to the original point, *"the autonomous personality is purified and can begin to live according to spiritual values, developing a relationship with the Higher Self, spiritual/divine".*[34] Astrological psychology provides a structured, practical way to understand one's

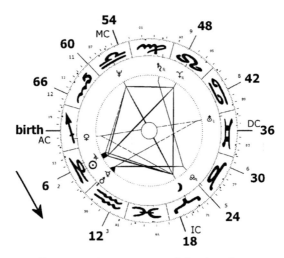

**Figure 2. Progression of the Age Point
shown in the Author's Natal Chart**

life journey during and after the ego-identifications begin to break down while one is still active and of the world.

Confusion and existential crises are caused, in part, by ego-identifications with our bodies, our occupations, our libidos and family roles as they begin to change drastically after age 40. In addition to the Age Point, the North Nodal point in the horoscope, its position in a given sign and house, can provide a hint to a more creative development beyond mid life.

> *"The North Node is rather like a compass needle in its ability to find the right way to improve our character. If we are going through periods of confusion in our life, the Node and its house positioning give the direction of the way ahead."*[35]

For example, if the North Node is in the 2nd house of possessions, resources, finances and a person is facing abandonment from a close business partner, then he contemplates his inner gifts – he can find new facets of his personality and weather the storm of this loss of relationship.

The movement of the Age Point forming aspects to transpersonal planets (Uranus, Neptune and Pluto) can highlight opportunities to transcend ego attachments associated with the relevant house. For example, if the Age Point is in the 10th house, the house of public image, career, managerial responsibility and Uranus is in square aspect to it, he may have shocking insights into how he conducts these affairs. It may come to awareness that he had been controlling and stifling, holding onto ways of handling subordinates for egoic reasons, i.e. to protect his image, to ensure conformity or to compel loyalty. By transcending and giving up this 'hold' on subordinates and seeing them as equals, he can remove the stubbornness of ego attachments using the insights given by the energy of Uranus.

When the Age Point conjuncts each house's Low Point, it is the closest to the center of the chart, which is our spiritual center (or Self). At these times *"we can most easily contact the energy of our true selves and the ideas that relate to our true purpose in this lifetime"*[36]. Here communion with the true Self can most easily occur. Each house Low Point symbolizes a minimum force of environmental influence upon the person and suggests a favorable time for introspection. (See Figure 3 – the Low Points are in the places where the outside lines are closest to the centre – near the middle of the houses).

If, for example, the Low Point is in the 11th house of associations, friendships, objectives, and ideals and if the person has a problem in these any of these areas, then he may find insights when contemplating these affairs and detaching from them. To do this, he could slow down his hectic life, retreat and not try to influence others, and thereby ease off from any outside pressures relating to friends,

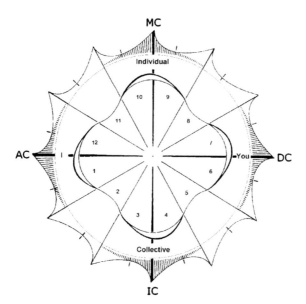

Figure 3. The Hubers' Dynamic Energy Curve

associates, and objectives. On the surface, it may be threatening to himself and others to act in this way, but in the long run, it can prove beneficial to hear the inner voice of the true self and perceive things not previously experienced for achieving an impartial viewpoint and finding a solution to an impasse. The more he is conscious of this developmental process, the more he can learn to become in contact with his higher spiritual nature – the higher self within us.[37]

But to be in contact with our 'transcendent ego', requires a conquering of ego attachments based on inner conflict and identification with a symbolic solution to how that conflict will be resolved. The challenging aspects in one's horoscope can highlight the conflict and if one can find a higher synthesis by, as Jolande Jacobi calls, the "uniting symbol", then one can find peace.

In astrological psychology the opposite poles in dualistic analysis of my horoscope is found with Neptune opposite the Moon (see Figure 4.) This creates acute tension between the collective ties to my family and the masses and my need to strive for my individuality. And the possible balance of these tensions through a 'third' pole is found in what is called the Encounter Axis (houses 1-7) where in spite of this grave battle between my individual needs against family

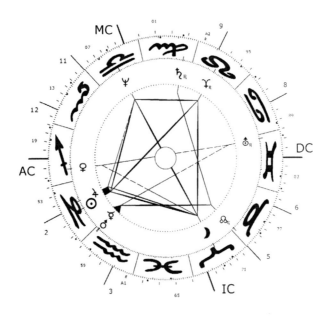

Figure 4. The Author's Natal Chart

demands, I must maintain contact with them and not look down on them. This dualism in my chart represents for me the conflict between my career ego and my unconscious ties to family and the only way to solve it is to keep the doors of communication with them open through encounter.[38a]

But whenever this symbol, in whatever form it takes, can manifest itself through diverse forms and manifest in the life of the person, the balance between the ego and the unconscious is restored.[38b] It could be the symbol of a spiritual guide, of Jesus or an avatar that one considers holy.

Jung describes the conscious development of the transcendent function as a way to find wholeness and balance needed to find reconciliation of a conflict and spiritual significance in later life. The process of individuation, as Jacobi describes, tries to achieve its goal by a natural production of symbols. It is work on the psyche in which the way is paved for a spiritual-ethical-religious order which is the consequence and not the content of the preparation, which must be chosen consciously and freely by the individual.

By the same method, by making the shadow conscious and expressed either through dream interpretation or through the use of active imagination in art, we can discover our unsocialized wishes and desires (close to the moon node chart in the Huber Method).[39,40] Becoming aware of inferior parts of ourselves in humility but not acting on them, lies, in part, along the path to individuation. But we should employ these functions with a sense of humor and patience as we embark on this more creative yet less competent journey.

At midlife a strange paradox exists: we have achieved competencies in the area of our involvement with the outer world (our dominant function) and lived out our potentials as identified in our radix chart, but now we must let our attachments to them go.[41] At this stage these functions of the personality become worn out from overuse and specialization.

Our task now is to deal with our unconscious complexes, motivations and conflicts – sub-personalities which can be revealed in the Huber astrological chart, e.g. as manifested by aspect patterns, specific aspects and unaspected planets. These conflicts and proclivities can be revealed in our dreams, fantasies and inner dialogues. By journaling with these forces within, we can see *"the false self slowly uncovered and we can begin to strip away the unnecessary constrictions of the ego that were established in ignorance simply to enable us to cope."*[42]

Journaling is an extremely personal and introspective process. Writing down dreams, linking the associations to conflicts within, and creating dialogues with our sub-personalities as revealed in the aspects of the astrological chart provides an infinite interplay of images always providing new insights. It is not easy because it is so interior and so lonely as the old scripts replay anew.

For example, in dreaming of parental figures, with my alcoholic father for example, I have found new insights arising out of my conflict with father. Not so much did I wage an external fight with him, rather I discovered an inner struggle to find my meaning and my significance instead of experiencing an inferiority complex. My impotent feelings (Neptune in house of career goal opposed Moon – see my chart in Figure 4) created compensations to build my sense of self worth (Sun square Neptune) and to confront authority through social work. My birth Sun is in Capricorn in the second house as a focal planet in an Achievement Square aspect pattern with the Moon opposed Neptune created the right dynamic for this complex to be resolved through an effort of will.

Growing up, my security was threatened by my father's erratic behaviors, which I internalized. After my parents' deaths, the traditional internalized mother and father arguing manifested by this Moon opposition Neptune prompted me to engage them in an inner dialogue as sub-personalities. Through written dialogue with them in my journal, I had layers of conversations through the years with each entity or sub-personality until they were transfigured into and absorbed by my Self. How this occurred was by taking responsibility for those conflicts with my parents as projected conflicts within myself and striving to find peace within myself so I could transcend the tension by yoga and meditation.

Another way to think about transformation and getting in touch with our true self is through identification with a strong symbol of change that is happening to us as evolution of society as a whole. Jonathon Zap develops the concept of a Singularity Archetype (my note: I associate it with today's Uranus square Pluto aspect), which represents an evolutionary movement manifesting with or without our conscious participation on a collective level. We find it occurs… as a *"rupture-of-plane event, usually threatening the survival of the individual and/or species. The event is a shock that disrupts the equilibrium of the body/physical world and also the individual/collective psyche. It is an ontological shock that will be viewed as the worst thing possible by the individual/collective ego."*[43]

Consider the global impact of global warming as an example with its violent changes in weather. As we prepare to allow the shell of ego identifications to die in us, we are preparing for our evolution by our collective/individual pursuits to prevent global warming.

IV. World Views in Collision

Established thought generated by universities and practiced by physicians in the Enlightenment of the 17th century sought physical causes for the diseases and anomalies that shortened longevity to half of what it is in the 21st century. Those who lived beyond 40 years were usually so grateful to God for preserving their lives that there was little reflection on the subtleties of their inner natures. An understanding of disease caused by the 'evil one' and by sin created a moralistic social order that perceived the 'flesh' as driving the mind to behaviors that were damned. Our scientific ancestors could only devote limited attention to the relationship between the body and mind to explain behavior. The biological sciences that dominated at the time were purposely focused on reducing pain and suffering of the general population. As such, astrological psychology was non-existent at that time. Since there was a biblical bias in Christian communities against reflection on the mind's conscious and unconscious motivations, divergent views of man were relegated to mystics and monasteries.

Tracing the emergence of astrological psychological thought through the writings of Leibnitz, Kant and later Jung, who established early foundations of understanding psychic structures and behaviors, we shall discover how marginalized they were. In the further development to this epistemology, the work of the esoteric astrologers such as Alice Bailey and Bruno Huber, who collaborated with Roberto Assagioli to support the study of the Self, we find no support from established institutions of higher learning.

Instead we find institutional support for the work of Descartes, Wundt and eventually the behaviorists whose focus was on the biological basis of behavior which penetrated well into to the 21st century.

This has led in the 21st century to a conflict of values, exacerbated by the breakdown of the authority of traditional knowledge by universal access to the internet, theoretical physics' field theory[45] and the emergence of astrological psychology out of the countercultural fringes of society into the mainstream of psycho-physical thought.[46]

A. Dualism vs. Pre-established Harmony

Rene Descartes' philosophy in the Enlightenment started the idea that the mind and body were split, holding that the mind is a nonphysical substance. Descartes clearly identified the mind with consciousness and self-awareness but distinguished this from the brain as the seat of intelligence. Hence, he was the first to formulate the mind-body problem. The seat of intelligence was believed to be in the brain and consciousness was seated in the mind.[47] Therefore, the mind and brain were not the same. But they did interact in a casual fashion through the pineal body, which is physically located between the eyes and up a few centimeters from the center of the brow line.

The pineal body's effect on behavior was little understood. Instead behavior was caused by the five senses (hearing, seeing, tactile, kinesthetic, and olfactory) creating impressions or images in the mind and motivating one to approach or avoid objects based on the positive or negative impressions they caused. These were subjective and added little to the objective knowledge base at the time. Physical causes were responsible for thought and emotions. Most scientific attention was on disease prevention, cure and alleviation of suffering among the masses. Little time was devoted to the psyche and the subjective study of the mind.

Descartes' view had consequences for later theoretical psychological development in which both mind and body had to be treated separately except where they interacted, but this caused problems for the Cartesians. Both mind and body had a materialistic and biological basis. And the sense impressions were subject to analysis only through the understanding of the activity of the brain.

Wilhelm Wundt (1880) was a structuralist.[48] He studied the structure or basic elements of the mind. Wundt professed an objective introspection by examining and measuring one's own thoughts and mental activities.

He trained volunteers to observe, analyze and describe their own sensations, mental images and emotional reactions. His goal was to break down behavior into basic elements. Wundt was one of the fathers of deterministic psychology. It evolved into the science of psychiatry. Thus, psychiatry was the analytical study of causes of disorders of the mind (mental), which had a biological basis.

Pre-established harmony, in philosophy, is the theory that mental and bodily experiences occur in tandem with each other, but without any type of causal interaction; it denies the interaction between the body and the mind. In other words, the mind and body are two independent phenomena but cannot be separated from one another – like two sides of a coin. The German philosopher Leibnitz believed that the mind and body did not need to interact as they were already synchronized through God's intervention – a pre-established harmony.[49] Leibnitz's philosophy was a counter to materialism and the dualism of Descartes. He thought that perception and consciousness cannot possibly be explained mechanically and hence could not be a physical process. He believed matter was infinitely divisible and therefore could not be concentrated to a truly single unit (1687). Thus, there could be no primary cause identified as related to an effect. He promoted and perceived virtue in studying unconscious influences and character types.

Immanuel Kant's view was that: *"the distinction between the unknowable noumena and phenomenal reality is the starting point of his critique of all metaphysical postulations, including those of the spiritualists"*.[50] Kant had provided the most succinct understanding of the philosophy which we endorse in his concept of *a priori*, subjective intuitions which were "given" in the sense of not learned. These intuitions could neither be caused by the activity of mind nor body. But at the same time they were relative to the space and time in which they were conceived. Kant went on to assert that human knowledge is possible only within the limits of the world of appearances; the world of noumena remains inaccessible to human reason. Phenomena can be studied by the world of appearances and knowledge gleaned from them and noumena can be studied by faith and belief.[51]

Two Schools

In my experience, these two schools developed into what predominates today's thinking on "cures" to mental problems.

On one hand, Cartesian dualism, Wundt's Structuralism and Neo-Freudian thought developed into behaviorism. Behavioral psychology as practiced in modern man looks at ego development by applying operant conditioning principles in the service of ego adaptation. If you find the cause of distorted thinking, then you can eliminate it by rehearsal and behavioral modification (Cognitive Behavioral Processing.)[52] Cause and effect of behaviors were directly applied by the empiricism of the behaviorists because units of behavior were easily quantified and empirically studied. There was a large body of empirical evidence supporting the theories of behaviorism. This is the prevailing method in Western institutions and hospitals in the 21st century.

On the other hand, we can trace from the historical roots in Leibnitz and Kant to the later attention given to the psychic structures of conscious/unconscious, first by Sigmund Freud, who championed the cause of a unified psychic system of conscious and unconscious which had structures of id, ego and superego. Jung's work on synchronicity and his understanding of individuation as a process of becoming whole driven by unconscious needs toward reconciliation of opposite psychic functions within played a huge role in complementing the acasual connecting principle by which astrology works. Added to this, theoretical physics field theory, which deals with the concept of quantum consciousness, legitimized the idea of a consciousness outside the body. It places memory in a field located not only in brain structures but in the sum total of the memory of man, in the collective unconscious.

Jungian psychology was based on conscious and unconscious factors, which through psychological complexes motivated behavior. The unit of study was the individual. His/her unconscious processes moved toward the goal of becoming whole, the process of individuation. Active analysis of unconscious contents especially through dreams, both personal and collective as they were played out in the person, provided the grist for the mill of the individuation process. Causes of behavior were not only instinctive and beyond experience but transpersonal. Dreams and their study were evidence that supported the existence of the unconscious contents to be a cause in any conscious behavior. The Jungian analytical method was teleologically based. It asserted that unconscious complexes motivate our behaviors, dreams provided hints about what the Self seeks, as well as dominant ego amalgamated functions in consciousness. Causes were deep within and led to a process of becoming a totally integrated human being through individuation.

Compatible with Jung's study of the Self, in which the total psyche was the unit of focus, Roberto Assagioli departed from Freud and introduced the movement of psychosynthesis that focused primarily on the Self. Psychosynthesis was described as follows: *"Beyond the limits of the ego lies the possibility of achieving spiritual transformation… the possibility of progressive integration of the personality around its own essential Self through the use of the will".*[53] His Psychosynthesis Institute, founded in Florence Italy, conducted experiments in models of consciousness that were receptive to higher, transpersonal activity working with the aid of the human will. This approach was appreciated much more in Europe, but was too difficult to operationalize for experimental psychology in the United States.

In America during the 20th century, the prevailing psychotherapies applied in hospital settings to the moral and healthy treatment of humans, focused on what was objective, could be time efficient, operationalized and manualized. Behaviorism had the upper hand and was used widely under the name of cognitive psychotherapies. As a Western concept in which strict controls had to be maintained at the expense of exploring the unconscious, these psychotherapies cured through time-limited interventions.

As applied psychological-political propaganda, behaviorism won out and could be used to teach armies to kill through the work of B. F. Skinner and classical conditioning: marines were taught in basic training how to respond to attacks by the enemy in a typical behaviorist manner – by splitting off negative emotions from the ego and becoming "killing machines". In basic training for combat in Vietnam, behavior modification techniques were use to depersonalize the enemy. Thus a collective psychology of the masses evolved with specific object of study being the human ego complex.

Jungian psychology could not be used by the collective political institutions to manipulate standard outcomes in behavior because it was too individualistic. Thus, Jungian analysis was subjected to the isolation of Institutes, which attracted its own followers who studied a longitudinal, spiritual journey into the deep recesses of the psyche. It required journaling with the concepts of the subjective reality of the subject and was not easily convertible into large empirical studies for consumption by popular psychology pundits.

Today the study of astrology and dreams is much more compatible with Jungian analysis because it is subjective, a priori based, acausal and communicates its validity through case studies. Astrology and dream theory, especially as espoused by Jung, had a strong teleological bent, a purpose for which it exists and a goal – wholeness or the reconciliation of opposites within the psyche.

The social consequence of applied psychology is essentially negative on supporting psychic significance to the individual. Ego psychology with its ego inflation, hubris, and self-aggrandizement is more practical when applied to the external world of cause and effect, as is apparent through empiricism. It can be grasped by the leaders of institutions for political ends. This is because in the application of social Darwinism that prevails in much political thinking, ego psychology and behaviorism are the most compatible with socio-political manipulation of the masses. Ego reduction, humility, and self-introspection are more applicable to the study of the individual and can't be applied to the masses. Jungian thinking is more compatible with these constructs.

In the final analysis of these two views of psychology, and the nature of man, both frameworks are needed. Developmentally, ego psychology is appropriate for youth and young adulthood until mid-life, when one is starting out in the world and building an identity. When psychic energies begin to wane and conscious functions seek wholeness, the use of astrological psychology is most compatible with the spiritual development that takes place at this stage of life. So in the context of the whole life cycle, both are needed in balance in order to control and develop some understanding of the individual in society and the mental problems he/she faces, especially as one develops through the complete life cycle as it extends well into the 80's in most developed countries.

B. Materialism vs. Spiritual Psychology

How we evolved to a materialistic value system in the academic psychology that is prevalent in Western countries is not a mystery. It is based on the historical confluence of religion as espoused by the protestant Calvinists and the development of capitalism with its work ethic.

The view that justice prevails when one does well in ones work and that God rewards His people based on their work ethic and accumulated wealth on earth represents the Calvinist and later the puritan view of civil society. John Calvin had the idea of predestination which was used as justification for idealizing those who were baptized, worked hard, accumulated wealth and were destined by God to go to heaven (the elect) and deprecating the poor who were not baptized and could/would not work as predestined for hell. Calvinism viewed worldly success as a blessing from God. Calvinists would engage in enterprising activities to prove to themselves their membership in the elect.[54]

Puritans who migrated to New England believed that common laws should reinforce the good, upright and sober person and those who engaged in vices (gambling, prostitution, drunkenness, and sloth) were destined for hell. The concept of the deserving poor was promoted by the idea that those who could not work but were poor for good reasons could get social support. But those who could work but would not were morally corrupt.[55] Therefore, if a person accumulates wealth through hard work, he or she is deemed a righteous person; on the contrary, if he/she does not work in the established way and have a degree of wealth, he/she is less perfect, less good and has a good chance for destiny in hell. These principles have become inculcated into the traditions and policies of the United States of America. As a society, we have looked at work as the highest form of access to the American Dream and as part of our constitutional right to "life, liberty and the pursuit of happiness". But this concept as promoted by our wealthy American society and made into policy through the concept of Manifest Destiny, has created a presumption of righteousness not appreciated by the rest of our global partners. One of the tenets of Manifest Destiny is that due to its uniqueness America may take morally questionable actions in the pursuit of virtuous goals. A case in point is the neo-conservative premise that we would go to war to spread democracy and capitalism to other countries, lately called the 'War on Terror'.[56]

The dichotomy of deserving wealthy nations versus the poorer, immoral and corrupt nations has evolved from these early founding assumptions of the moral righteousness of hard work and its destined rewards in heaven to a form of imperialism. As countries have become more interdependent, these perceptions are actually seen to be due to a false hubris of the Western globalized, perception which has its roots in materialism. Even though wealthy countries pour money into poorer ones, the poor do not love the rich ones more and neither does God. One does not get rewarded in temporal life for good works.[57]

When we base our perception of reality on only the Cartesian view, the behaviorists and materialism, we are left morally bankrupt. Although we are engorged with empirical studies that justify the dominance of these philosophies as profitable and they are promoted as objective truths that govern our Western world, there is no justification for a rich society that exploits other countries and protects its 'rights' through military interventions.

However, when we presume to promote a psychology which identifies the unconscious and conscious psyche as an object of study, we are confronted with universal symbols, myths and stories which have their basis in the world's major religions. This psychology is a subjective approach and does not thrive on self-interest. This effort then, is the focus of this work and we shall promote a spiritual dimension in the psychology of humans because to do so incorporates what is important to the development of the Self – the subjective entity in the psyche that is the source of faith, belief and wholeness. What is important to human spiritual evolution is building of love and compassion as the creator has promised. One can create good karma through love because it calibrates at the highest level of consciousness that makes it worth striving for in this life.[58] But the new paradigm is to love and to work and not be attached to the outcome of being saved or being given grace by God.

This higher karmic consciousness is based on devotion to equanimity and love. But let us not think that our projections of what we think is 'good' will be salvation for our souls because what is good is relative. As Richard Tarnas points out in *Cosmos and Psyche* "because *any meaningful purpose the human mind perceives in the universe does not exist intrinsically in the universe but is constructed onto it by the **human** (my emphasis) **mind**. This privileging of the human, the anthropocentric projection is the subtle but prodigious form of human aggrandizement.*[59]

C. The Symbolic Life – Justification for the Belief in Dream Study and Astrology

Any psychology that proposes to cover the broad subject of the unconscious and its contents, and then refutes tenets of American behavioral psychology that has been dominant in the 21st century, must have justification for its assertions. It is important for us to **believe** in working with unconscious symbolism through astrology and the self-study of dreams. For without this belief, we cannot recommend the study of our discipline in a materialistic world. In psychological and physical health belief plays a vital role. Just to prove how important it is to believe in and have a commitment to these disciplines is revealed by Herbert Benson who notes that it has been estimated that belief plays an important and primary role in the resolution of 75% of health problems that do not respond to specific treatments.[60]

Belief in the importance of the interpretation of dreams as vital to good health, individuation and psychological well-being is essential. C. G. Jung proposed that dreams are an involuntary psychic process and emanate from psychological complexes in the unconscious. He believed and devoted his professional career to the belief that dreams offer compensatory functions to our ego identifications, emotional correction and contributions toward problem solving in life.[61]

Nowlin (1965) studied REM (rapid eye movement) sleep which is usually associated in dreaming with the emotional content of dreams. He monitored REM in dreaming subjects in a controlled study and discovered that chest pain is correlated with dreams involving strenuous physical activity and those involving fear, anger and frustration. We can surmise from Nowlin's study that the subjects' lack of awareness of the content of their dreams and their lack of ability to modify their behavior based on the knowledge imparted by their dreams led to health issues with chest pain.[62]

Dream images have contents that are symbolic. As Jung explains, *"A term or image is symbolic when it means more than it denotes or expresses. It has a wider 'unconscious' aspect – an aspect that can never be precisely defined or fully explained. This peculiarity is due to the fact that, in exploring the symbol, the mind is finally led towards ideas of a transcendent nature, where our reason must capitulate.*"[63]

Humankind has had a universal awareness of dreams since the beginning of time. The language of the unconscious is represented by dream symbols and has comprised images that depict potentials and outcomes of mythic stories. Conscious and unconscious minds exist everywhere and are the reservoir for personal and collective information/thought forms, the expression of which is dreams.

In order to understand how symbolic images activate our personalities, we need to first understand the topographical levels of the psyche: See Figure 1.[64]

---

1. Personal consciousness – ordinary awareness

2. Personal unconscious – unique to the individual psyche

3. Objective psyche – universal structure in mankind (collective unconscious)

4. Collective conscious – cultural awareness of shared values and forms.

It should be noted that the specialized structures of the personal parts of the psyche, both conscious and unconscious, are four: ego, persona, shadow and syzygy (paired groupings) animus/anima. The archetype of the Self is known as the central archetype of order.[65]

Figure 1. Levels of the Psyche

Second, understand that dreams in the form of symbolic images located in the personal unconscious and objective psyche emanate from two types of general structures: complexes and archetypal images.

"Complexes are groups of related images in the personal unconscious held together by a common emotional tone. Associations tend to cluster around a certain theme, such as associations with the mother – called a mother complex."[66]

"(Complexes) are formed on an archetypal matrix in the objective psyche. At the core of every complex is an archetype. The ego is formed upon the archetypal core of the Self; (for example) behind the personal mother complex is the Great Mother archetype."[67]

The Great Mother archetype is directly associated with to the astrological qualities of the Moon, representing its nurturance function, and Saturn, representing its security function.

Within the objective psyche there are archetypes and archetypal images whose number cannot be precisely stated but which correlate to the archetypes of the planets, which have dynamic activating power through images dramatized in dreams, thus influencing our conscious behavior through dream-ego activity.

For example, in dreaming of being visited by Jesus what is happening could be as follows: the universal divinity symbol in the objective psyche activates the God complex (which we assume exists in our individual example), which in turn creates a living dream image of Jesus that inspires the dream ego and thus influences the subject's conscious behavior. The binary nature of the archetype of divinity is associated with the astrological Sun. On one hand, the Sun represents the conscious ego; on the other hand, the Sun is associated with the unconscious Self.

Jung asserts that the objective psyche generates our symbols. *"The dogma of religions is seen as a condensation or distillation of the sacred history of (the God) myth – that of the divine being and his/Her deeds."*[68] Dreams of contact with God are recorded in the Koran, the Bible and other great books.

Dreams of the God experience can tap into existing aspects of psychological complexes in the unconscious of certain individuals. For these individuals, the God archetype is a manifestation of the astrological Sun symbol with psychological states of willfulness, creativity, vitality and confidence on the positive side; and pride, conceit and arrogance on the negative side. (See Appendix 2 under Leo the Sun sign.) It can manifest as narcissistic traits in its most pathological forms. But it can also inspire and create experiences for the individual of union with the Self (God). In both cases, it is known as a God complex in the personal unconscious. This experience of a complex in which God is the focus of a person's life journey is an example of a process Jung called individuation. But a person can be so devoted to experience spiritual union with God that he/she may go to extremes of spiritual discipline so as to go against his/her own health and will. Even though the experience of this God complex may lead to the experience of mystical union with God, it can be devastating to the external ego-laden world of that person's reality. There is always a risk when one indentifies with an archetype that ones ego can become inflated and/or one experiences rejection; as one submits to a collective, objective symbol instead of individual, personal symbols such of submission to secular authority.

Jung explains the relationship between the objective psyche and the individual psyche by the following:

"...If we wish to understand the dogma, we can for example, consider the myths of Near and Middle East that underlie Christianity... And then the whole of myth (is seen) as an expression of universal disposition in man. This disposition I have called the collective unconscious, the existence of which can be inferred only from individual phenomenology. In both cases (following religions of Christianity or Islam, for example), the investigator comes back to the individual, for what he is all the time concerned with are certain complex thought-forms, the archetypes, which must be conjectured as the unconscious organizers of our ideas."[69]

Thus, there are collective and personal symbols, one uniting and influencing the other. These form universal patterns or motifs which come from the objective psyche of the collective unconscious and are the basis of the content of religions, mythologies, legends and fairy tales. They create thought-forms or archetypes that are unconscious/conscious forces that organize human behavior. They have an innervating effect on our psyches, organizing our thoughts and letting the instincts carry them into action. The collective becomes indivualized through the activation of complexes in the personal unconscious.[70]

Each person lives by an autobiographical history and personal myth. The drama of his/her myth is portrayed in dreams as they interact with everyday events and the unconscious complexes within. Most of the time we are not aware of the unconscious motivation that comes from our personal myth. Each culture of the earth lives by a collective myth as well as a history. There is value in a single-subject study of our dreams, which speaks in symbols to our personal myth, over a lifetime. This can lead to greater self-realization of the meaning of life; without it one is caught up in a meaningless chaos of collective life.

Astrology has, for thousands of years, represented a system of archetypal and symbolic language that is related to individual lives and personal myths.

For example, the 'hero' is an archetype operating in the sign Aries as the Mars symbol. (See Appendix 2.) As an archetype constellated with positive and negative energies in the personal unconscious, this archetype 'lives' as a complex in the personal unconscious of many soldiers today. As an archetype, it has both negative a positive psychological states:

Positive: To assert, initiate, vitalize and act

Negative: Aggression, violating the rights of others, hostility when thwarted, egocentric and primitive when with others.[71]

When one is living the myth of the hero one can go off to war and fight the enemy with conviction (especially if his/her culture and experience supports the culture of guns and weaponry) and prevail against the projected enemy. In the development of the hero myth, one has tests (i.e. overcoming fear of death), passes these tests with difficulty and finally surmounts them; yet has to guard against excessive egocentric pride that can lead to a fall. A person can follow the path of the hero but no real person can embody the range of possibilities in the hero archetype. Many of our soldiers fighting in Iraq and Afghanistan believe they are 'warriors' and that archetype has a vivifying effect on their identities – but once their duty is done, they have to find a modification of that symbolic identity to live out in civilian life or be cast into depression and chaos with a lost identity. This transition to the moral code of civil society after war is difficult. The reformulation of the hero comes up against the issues of morality, killing and the Venusian archetype constellating love, forgiveness and relatedness. This transition is very difficult to cross and to maintain. When faced with these transitions, dreams reveal the conflicts between the positive and negative psychological states of the Mars/Venus archetypes... being attacked and fighting vs. loving and longing for equal union, the need to relate vs. the active intention to do harm. Psychological astrology can give symbolic information and make the inner conflicts and dreams of returning soldiers comprehended.

Collective symbols are found everywhere, are universal to the earth, and found in all cultures. They are the archetypes. But men and women live out symbols as energized by their deeds in life. Dreams capture these actions in a mythic pattern as they dramatize the destiny of the ego leading to the real Self.

Psychological astrology identifies our motivations through the aspect patterns and our life goals that are synchronized to the timing of significant events in the individual's personal myth. That inner conflicts exist universally and are revealed through dreams as one comes up against the mythological dramas in everyday life is the basis of my discovery. Astrology as revealed through the planetary archetypes shows up in dreams as psychological states and dominates and motivates our conscious thoughts and actions. This important fact justifies the belief both in astrology and in dream self study.

D. Mind-Body Interaction in life and death:

On July 31,1999, I had a visitation. I was sleeping alone in my bed. My wife, Judy, was attending a summer dance program with my daughter Miranda in Carlisle, Pa. I awoke to find a silhouette of a dark heavy male figure standing near my bed. I could sense a profound foreboding with its presence as the sensation of increased humidity of the bedroom was palatable. I was terrified, maybe for the first time in years. When I finally got back to sleep, I was again awakened by a phone call. My mother-in-law, Ruth, called to tell me that my father-in-law, Tom, is gone, deceased, passed on.

When Judy returned from Carlisle, the shocking death of her father created a drive in her to communicate with her father's spirit – a reunion of sorts since she had been away during his passing. She researched and found that the famous medium George Anderson[72] was going to give a cold reading for enrolled people at a Holiday Inn on Long Island, New York in September of that year. My son, Tom, took Ruth and Judy to that reading. George Anderson told Judy, *"I have a message from someone in uniform (Tom Bushby was a World War II veteran who was stationed in the Pacific) to his one and only".* Judy taped the message of George and knew it was meant for her, Tom's only child and daughter.

When Ruth died in 2011, Judy and I attended her passing. She died in bed at her home. It was a wonderful, sacred moment for me and a privilege to be with her during that moment. I had a dream about Ruth following her passing; the dream image of her bound like a shadow on Judy's back as she gathered up Ruth's precious belongings. It was as if Ruth was attempting to enter the earthly plane and commune with Judy by attaching her spirit to her as she was working.

When the body dies, does the person's mind evaporate like water on a hot day? The mind-body dichotomy of Descartes, as has been described, had been dominating philosophical thought since the Enlightenment. This prevailing view has created the sciences of the body and the mind separately. And led to the conclusion that once the body dies, the brain which is the seat of intelligence dies too. The new view espoused by psychologist Dr. Gary E. Swartz does not presume that the mind and body are separate, but they are interconnected. Furthermore, once the body dies, the intelligence and consciousness of the brain can live on even though the body in its corporal form no longer exists.

Furthermore, the mind and body interact and are part of the whole psychic system. Consciousness emerges from the unaware, undeveloped instinctual unconscious mind. But, mind-consciousness is separate from the brain. There is substantial anecdotal evidence that when people are declared brain dead the organs of perception live on and "intelligence" is not seated in the organic brain. *"Consciousness exists independently from the brain. It does not depend on the brain for its survival."*[73]

Jung's dissertation for his medical degree was on the subject "On the Psychology and Pathology of So-Called Occult Phenomena" (1902). Jung disclosed to the world what his chosen concentration would be. He had mediums on his mother's side of the family and had experience directly throughout the course of his life work with them (Miss Miller's fantasies). Although he at first saw spiritualism experiences as the result of autonomous complexes, he later refined his view that archetypes were rooted in a trans-psychic reality that was on one end matter and on the other spirit.[74]

At the end of his life, in *Memories Dreams and Reflections*, Jung interpreted certain dreams of the dead as actual visits of the dead to the dreamer. Although he did not write the following dream as a visitation from his wife Emma, Jung dreamed her as young woman with a face neither sad or joyful but rather objectively wise and understanding. She was beautiful and commissioned her portrait for him which satisfied him to a great extent; for it was evidence of his completed individuation – the total integration of thinking and feeling by the Self.[75]

In May of 1960, Jung conceded:

> *"We may therefore expect postmortal phenomenon to occur which must be regarded as authentic. Nothing can be ascertained about existence outside time... But this does not exclude the possibility that there is existence outside time, which runs parallel with existence inside time. Yes we may simultaneously exist in both worlds, and occasionally have intimations of a two-fold existence. But what is outside time is, according to our understanding, outside change. It possesses relative eternity."*[76]

When the body dies with the brain, the mind with its seat of personal consciousness still continues. This is substantiated in research of mediums contacting the spirit world.[77]

What information is transmitted from a parallel existence that runs simultaneously with our own? The deceased person's *"consciousness: contains the personal archetype/myth an individual lived before death".*

These archetypes live on also as part of the field of energy in a total psychic system of the deceased individual in the form of complex energy constellations that have emotional valence.

Most medium contact with the "other side" involves evoking the archetype or symbol the person lived while on the earthly plane. That elicits a response consistent with personal characteristics of the deceased person when contact is made. I refer to the work of Allan Botkin, PSY.D. In his work with induced after-death communication found that providing eye movement desensitization and reprocessing (EMDR) to combat veterans evoked communication with their deceased combat buddies who shared the common focal trauma of death in war. He found that the traumatic death incidents were *"remembered and acknowledged by the deceased victims themselves and communicated to the living."*[78] In many of Botkin's cases, the deceased reassured the living that in spite of a violent death in war, they are at peace and totally congruent with the death experience. This was therapeutic for the survivors in Botkin's caseload and a great relief. The fact that they (both the living and the dead) shared a common trauma was the personal archetype (the Pluto archetype in astrology) that brought them together in a common energy field and elicited an interaction with the living and the deceased.

I propose that the consciousness that carries on does so by information that is stored in the netherworld. Information is transmitted to the living whether it is the death trauma information or a life pattern motif. An example of this transmission of information after death is that memory that is preserved with the soul in reincarnation. There is documented evidence of small children who identify with a family and feel that they were part of that family in a previous life, once they are capable of language and communicating. Reincarnation research studied 40 children who chose to be re-incarnated into a new body with a new family and 'remember' their previous incarnation.[79] To 'choose' to be born again at a specific time and location demonstrates the link between reincarnation and astrology. For the way this secret information is conveyed is a stamp on a newly incarnated soul. It shows up as aspect patterns and ego placements in the nodal horoscope.[80] Of course, this flies in the face of empiricism because these truths cannot be replicated in large numbers with statistical methods. However, the truth in this single subject design can yield the validity and reliability of this approach if one is open to it.

E. The Breakup of Dimensions of Time and Space

At Merrill-Palmer Institute in Detroit, Michigan in the winter of 1969, I cast my first I Ching. The *I Ching*, or *Book of Changes* is a Confucian oracle. In the Wilheim-Baynes translation, the text I received for my first interpretation was Hexagram 61, Inner Truth, line four which says, "Before the full moon the team horse goes astray. No blame." In the commentary it stated that one must be humble in the face of enlightenment and be single minded. Renounce factionalism and be like a horse that goes straight ahead without looking from side ways to its mate – that is the only way to retain the inner freedom that helps one onward. That single-minded purpose, belonging to no group, institution or association was my path. That attitude helped me to pursue my own thoughts, philosophy and direction in my life and prepared me for my own lonely, mystical recovery. I have been a medium through my dream life, receiving personal spiritual wisdom. Only now can I ponder the transmission of this legacy of great truths to others.

Time and space dimensions in the material world operate by the laws of physics. Empirical science is a valid approach to truth on the physical plane. Physical law generalizations are mostly collective in nature and apply to general populations or to the sample under study, but no further.

Time and space continuums of the dream world and astrology apply to individual psychic energy which is not bound by physical time and space boundaries. But dreams and astrology operate by the law of correspondences, not empiricism.[81]

Mystics have for centuries found that time and space break down when one reaches spiritual attainment of enlightenment through meditation.[82] One can have the subjective experience of making time stand still or move forward or backward in time. Para-psychological abilities such as clairvoyance and precognition show up during and after meditation exercises. Contemplation induces receptivity to the correspondences that reflect personal, social movements and *"great global transformations that open up awareness of God operating in the world. Emancipatory movements (the Arab spring of 2011) that coincide with angular aspects of Uranus, Pluto and Neptune"* are examples of synchronistic events coinciding with aspects among the trans-Saturn planets.[83] Dreams that show up at times in a person's life coinciding with important aspects of 'Age Point' progressions are openings to inspiration and to glimpses of our developmental growth cycles. These synchronistic events imply that significant autobiographical events are guided by a higher spiritual consciousness.

Dreaming and meditation are both thought forms that escape the time space continuum. Minds can communicate with minds from the past, in the present, or from the future in all places on earth, through meditation, mediums and/or through dreams. In *The Afterlife Experiments* Gary E. Swartz found, *"information (from mediums) was consistently received that can best be described as coming from live souls... of deceased people."*[84]

Astrological aspects act as timing mechanisms and triggers in the lives of peoples and nations. The life events of the people (such as getting a new career, marriage, retirement,) are announced by dreams in which the ego undergoes transformation and change in its identity pattern.

V. Astrological Psychology

Astrology helped me to identify how to time my life events from the very beginning of my search for the right path in my early twenties. When to advance and when to retreat was a new value for a Western raised man who had been indoctrinated that progress and achievement is all there is to do at every opportunity. You would not stop – 'he who hesitates is lost'. Astrology also represented to me a way to find my authentic self. I knew early in my studies that identification with my rising sign or ascendant, Sagittarius was only the superficial or social me. To find my true self, I had to learn to identify with my Sun, its placement in Capricorn, its aspects and finally to transcend these to find the peace and silence within. What was crucial for my development of a systematic approach to astrology and psychology was my diploma work with Dr. Maureen Demot. Dr. Demot was South African and a Jungian astrologer. I took her course in 1999 and 2000. She taught the correspondences between different Jungian structures in the psyche and astrological symbols. For example:

Birthchart = the psyche

Moon and Venus = anima in man

Sun and Mars = animus in women

Planets = archetypes or primordial instinctual image

Elements of water, earth, fire and air = functions of feeling, sensing, intuition and thinking respectively

Collective consciousness = planets and sign represent symbolically collective psychic contents common to all humankind

Collective unconscious = planets and signs

Complex = aspects, especially challenging ones and aspect patterns

Ego and Self = Sun and midheaven relate to the ego; the Sun also relates at a higher level to the Self.

Disassociation = unconnected aspect patterns

Extraversion = planets in positive signs, north and east hemispheres

Introversion = planets in negative signs, south and west hemispheres

After Dr. Demot's death in 2001, I had been floundering with the approach she had founded because there was not an association or school which coherently focused all these concepts. Then in 2008, I found the Huber school of Astrological Psychology which combined the works of astrology with the work of Roberto Assagioli. Assagioli and Huber combined the analysis of the astrological chart with the goal of finding the true Self, a super-ordinate goal of Self discovery I had been looking for. This was a higher level of organization than was provided for by either school alone and combined with Demot's Jungian astrology was the answer for me.

Traditional astrology had seen man as a passive victim of fate determined by the nature of planets in aspect in his/her natal chart. Some proponents had determined that there is a causal relationship between the planets and our physical bodies and thus our fates. Johannes Kepler saw the mechanism of this action through the concept of the Music of the Spheres, which is a musical-geometrical influence of the planets in respect of the birth horoscope.[85]

This new field of astrological psychology has changed the view of astrology and man in the Western world. As this excerpt from Wikepedia explains:

> *"Astrological Psychology is a recent product of the cross-fertilization of the fields of astrology with depth psychology, humanistic psychology, and transpersonal psychology. It uses the horoscope and the archetypes of astrology to inform the psychological understanding of an individual's psyche… Bruno Huber & Louise Huber developed their own method of astrological psychology, referred to as the Huber Method, with links to Roberto Assagioli's work with psychosynthesis."*

My application of astrological psychology to understanding my development has three separate roots:

1. From the early work of Carl Jung which led to the process of integration of opposites in the psyche and Dr. Maureen Demot who combined astrology and Jungian psychology.[86]

2. From the psychological synthesis of the planets and the establishing of the Huber School which used principles of psychosynthesis.

3. Dane Rudhyar's integration of the transpersonal planets which represented the individuation process.[87]

When Carl Jung was investigating the symbolic meaning of his dreams and the active imagination just before World War I, he was confused by the horror of the images he perceived. He investigated his dreams and fantasies and came across mythical figures that have been passed down to him from the bible, and the collective unconscious of his ancestors. Jung's dreaming of the blind Salome and prophet Elijah were figures in dialogue with his dream-ego. They corresponded to complexes in Jung's personal unconscious, namely Eros and Logos respectively.[88]

Eros was creativity; Logos was reasoning. I drew an association in the images pictured in dreams to the gods that were attached to heavenly figures mapped out in the stars i.e. Eros is Pluto and Logos is Uranus. For Jung these forces in the psyche, Eros and Logos had to be united in order for wholeness to be achieved in the individual's life. This was a process, which culminated in individuation, reconciliation of the opposites in one's psychic system. For example, if one followed logic too rigidly (logos), one's creativity (eros) would be stifled. On the physical plane if one is motivated by Eros and does not follow Logos, then one could be pulled into moral decay.

The heavenly figures in astrology come from a complex of opposing images or archetypes in the collective unconscious. It was these mental images that brought about astrological symbols. The planets represent a series of opposing images or archetypes. These archetypes are 'downloaded' from the collective unconscious to the personal unconscious of individuals. The horoscope represents the organizing structure of the psyche, the Self, which constellates the images as symbolized by the planets' archetypes into our conscious awareness through dreams, fantasies, traits and actions. The interpretation of the horoscope involved the synthesis of oppositional tendencies in one's soul. The journey around the circle of the horoscope represents a developmental journey leading to individuation.

Further mature development was brought about through relationships between the sexes. Jung analyzed astrological aspects between planets in couples and he could predict choice of a mate in marriage based on, for example, the conjunction of planets of moon and sun in two charts of a man and a woman represented a complete, syzygy or union of opposites.[89] It was through this union between a man and a woman that satisfactory psychological development could flower.

The work of Bruno and Louise Huber started the Huber School of astrological psychology in Switzerland in 1962. The Hubers used tenets of the Italian psychiatrist Roberto Assagioli to develop a system of astrological psychology leading to psycho-integration and transcending the ego through psychosynthesis.

The ego as a psychic structure was associated with three planets: Saturn, the Moon and the Sun. In psychosynthesis, these ego planets are transformed to a higher level beyond just security, a sense of belonging and willful effort. The ego is no longer the pinnacle of psychological achievement for the individual. In fact it is subservient to the Self. By identification with the Self, the needs of the ego are transcended so that a synthesis occurs, resembling Jung's individuation process.

This had foundations in the Theosophical work of Alice Bailey and was the beginning of what would later become the Astrological Psychological Association in England.[90]

An important astrological psychology contributor was Dane Rudhyar who also took Jung's psychological concepts and applied them to astrology. Rudhyar found that from horoscopes he could discover the structure of character and enhance psychological self-understanding. From this he discovered that a person's mental difficulties could be found through the analysis of complexes in the natal horoscope. Thus astrology could further discern psychological traits, conflicts and solutions and satisfy the non-neurotic basis of self-understanding.[91]

With the work of Jung, Huber and Rudhyar, the groundwork had been laid for further development of astrological psychology. Astrological psychology does not attribute the planets as causing behavior in man's everyday life, nor is life on earth dictated by the position of the stars, but the relationship is defined as part of a super-implicate order. As Keiron Le Grice explains, the planetary archetypes

"are indeed multidimensional universal principles that pertain to nature and to the cosmos as a whole and are not just to an interior encapsulated psyche, we would expect to find evidence of these creative principles at the cosmological, geological, and biological levels of reality too. We would expect that these principles are not just experienced intrapsychically as archetypal images in dreams and fantasies, or in the exceptional occurrence of synchronicities in the external world, but that they are also consistently evident across all levels of the universe-in, for example, the processes that give birth to galaxies, that form solar systems, that formed the Earth, and that are manifest, too, in the plant and animal kingdoms. We would expect, in short, that these principles are indeed universal, that their effects, their signatures are seen everywhere."[92]

Aspect patterns in the horoscope are part of the universal reflection of this principle of formative causation and super-implicate order of the cosmos that is ubiquitous. Astrological psychology then, is perceived as a tool to help identify a person's attributes and potential in being congruent with this order. For example, a psychological astrologer might use a horoscope to see if the individual possesses specialized mental abilities based on their Mercury position and aspects to it as reflected in the attributes of Mercury in all its manifestations.

I have used references to Bruno and Louise Huber's work in astrological psychology. The Astrological Psychology Association in England (APA) has a school and a method that uses three horoscopes or charts: the radix, birth or natal chart; the house chart which identifies the effects of early conditioning and the environment; and the Moon Node or nodal chart which is a mirror image of karmic legacy from our past and manifests in the unconscious psyche as, for example, the Jungian concept of the shadow shows up in our lives as an inferior aspect of our behaviors. (See John Grove's Huber 3-chart presentation in Appendix 1). The Huber Method is a system that is compatible with Jungian theory explicated here. The APA approach goes beyond just a description of individual character traits to developing a real tool for reflective investigation of one's own psyche and psychological and spiritual development. It is developmental across the life cycle and demonstrates convincingly, how Age Point progressions manifest in different motivations and needs at different maturity levels of the individual.[93]

The unique perspective of our approach combines Jungian techniques of dream analysis and relates these to dynamics of chart interpretation using the Huber Method to do character study, timing of developmental events in the life of the person and the identification and resolution of intra-psychic conflict.

There are three essential applications of this approach that I use:

1. Developmental challenges are revealed by the critical times when the Age Point transits planets that are in aspect to one another, or to other sensitive points in the chart; thus creating a crisis of consciousness.[94] This process is paralleled in the timing of certain dreams which usually identify the crisis to the native's dream ego as he/she comes up against losses or challenges. Personal identity losses (family role), occupational identity losses, and physical body losses through illness usually come up in dreams. The recording and amplification of dreams, and the date they are dreamed are correlated with critical periods or crossing points and aspects of the Age Point. By this synchronistic correspondence, I can identify meaningful ways in which the Self is preparing one for losses, which has implications for healing and personal transcendence.

2. I relate the nodal chart to Jung's concept of the shadow in the psyche. A shadow projection is autonomous, has an emotional nature and accordingly an obsessive or, better, possessive quality.[95] A shadow projection as identified in a dream is an image that can be depicted in a drawing. If the dreamer can see parts of him/herself in the shadow figure from the dream, then her task is to take responsibility for her shadow nature and bring it to conscious awareness. When the shadow is unconscious, we project it onto a scapegoat, like the way Jews were treated by the Germans in World War II. The Germans projected all their negative traits that they did not acknowledge and put them on the Jews. This shadow conflict has a direct bearing on psychological health and healing of modern man as most people are unconscious of their shadow, their dream life or it's implications in finding enemies in their projections. If we begin to understand the sometimes disturbing impulses coming from deep within our psyche, our capacity for evil and how the task of our time on earth is to discover how to heal the dualistic split within ourselves by taking responsibility: then we can live a much more peaceful life. The nodal chart also refers to our reincarnated soul in this lifetime and reflects desires coming from previous lives and their traumatic complexes of energy.[96]

3. The house chart reveals how the environment, early development and education influenced and continues to affect our development. The house chart does not compel us to react to its influence. When we realize that our motivations come from our conditioning as revealed by the aspect patterns in this horoscope, we can stop running after what others expect us to do and quietly reflect on what our authentic self's desires are instead. Crises of growing pains in the individual occur when the Age Point contacts sensitive parts (natal planets) of this horoscope.[97]

For astrological psychology using the Huber Method the reader is referred to the APA website www.astrologicalpsychology.org.

VI. Dreams' origin and influence on personal development

I will digress here to justify the use of these personal dreams as a scientific method much like an anthropological study. The validity of dreams having inner images that guide the ego to truth resembles a naturalistic observation, not unlike Dr. Jane Goodall's observations of the great apes in the Congo. Although its conclusions are subjective and a single subject design, it serves as a unique example for others who are similarly inclined to follow.

What follows are depictions from my own dreams and I want the reader to be aware that I am fully conscious of the subjective nature of the dreaming psyche. But without a connection to one's dreams, life is not rich at all. We cannot fill our coffers with the meaning and significance that dreams lend when the materialistic, deterministic existence of so many persons today – who are driven to drugs, false identities and ultimately in some cases to suicide – dominate our conscious focus.

In June of 1973, before I went to Yemen for training in Arabic language and teaching English as a foreign language, I dreamed terrible dreams. Dead bodies were everywhere, corpses littered streets I had never seen, skeletons *en masse* were polluting the landscape of cities; these came to me night after night before I left the US. Some of these ghastly images still intrude on my consciousness today, some forty years later. I realize now but did not know then that these were precognitive dreams. I relate these killings to destruction in the Middle East, exploitation and violence during the twentieth and early twenty first centuries. The hostage crisis of 1979, the 1988 war between Iraq and Iran, the Gulf War of 1990, 2001 attack on the World Trade Center, the wars in Iraq and Afghanistan from 2011 to 2014 these were actual events that my dreams were illustrating.

I recorded these dream images in my dream journal. But as a young Peace Corps volunteer in 1973, I ignored those dreams at the time. I was like a brooding crusader with a mission and nothing would deter me from going to Oman and volunteering with the Peace Corps with optimism. But these old series of dreams, a presage of the future, beg the question – where did they come from and who owns the dream content? Is it from me or is it knowledge from a collective awareness that is out there in some electronic field of knowledge transmitted to my dreaming mind? The answer I believe is that I was picking up from the collective unconscious images of what was to happen in that geo-political inferno.

Carl Jung determined that dreams play a role in highlighting the individual's psychological complexes/archetypes in his/her personal unconscious.[98] The definition of a psychological complex is that it is an unconscious encapsulation of two opposing feeling states, each with a valence of positive or negative feelings. The complex dynamic generates psychic energy from the unconscious. Some examples are: independence vs. the need to be taken care of; assertion vs. passivity or aggression; suppression of thoughts and feelings vs. expression of thoughts and feelings; in human produced trauma, the need to relate vs. the intention to do harm. On more archetypal levels dreams represent a mother complex (stay with mother or leave); father complex (listen to authority and do not question it or strike out on your own); God complex (spiritual fanaticism or find the God/Self within you). The unconscious structures, the shadow, animus and anima archetypes are activated by dreams and take the form of projections onto people by the conscious ego.

Dreams play a role in transient ego identity attachments. They can have a compensatory or balancing role in the psyche between the conscious ego and the Self which generates all dream content. A trigger event usually confronts the ego which stimulates an already existing complex/archetype in the unconscious to produce a dream. When the dream occurs, the ego identity of the individual involved is infused with images from these complexes/archetypes coming through the dreams.

For example, one is fighting with various unknown figures of the same sex in a dream. If the images are projected onto a real person, the whole effort is wasted. However, through self-analysis, *"if the ego image is understood that it may alter depending upon which complex (or combination of complexes) the ego uses for a dominant identity; then it is fairly easy to see where in shadow projections for example, the ego feels fairly justified in actively liking someone or not liking someone (usually the same sex as the ego) who embodies qualities that (to everyone other than the person doing the projecting) are present in the ego image of the patient."* Thus, the dream images can have a compensatory or opposite effect on the ego – driving it to balance out the dreamt images representing one side of the conflict to the other side if the projection is withdrawn[99]. The goal of uniting these opposing inner forces, led by the Self, is to prepare the individuation process, a purpose of the Self by which duality is transcended and union/peace is achieved. The individuation process actually prepares one for death which is the ultimate combining and transcendence of opposites: to acceptance of death as the goal of life.

So I feel it is important to study dreams and they are the key to self understanding as well as gleaning information about our world. My intention is to present a practical method of recording the types of dreams, and interpretations of them.

Dreams represent the "royal road to the unconscious" (Freud). As Ole Vedfelt indicates in *Dimensions of Dreams*, there are 4 types:

1. Dreams represent an unconscious reaction to a conscious situation.

2. Dreams represent a situation that springs from a conflict between conscious and unconscious.

3. Dreams represent a tendency in the unconscious to strive for changing the conscious attitude (or compensating for it).

4. Dreams represent unconscious processes in which no connection to consciousness can be made.[100]

Ira Progoff has indicated that the timing of dreams is important.[101] In sections below, we will introduce a daily log for a person to keep track of the timing of dreams related to it.

How to keep a dream log or diary for interpretation

I attended two of Ira Progoff's "Intensive Journal Workshops", one time in 1971 as a graduate student and another in 2001, four days after the death of my mother. In 2001 I had registered for the course to be held in Pittsburgh, Pa. on February 17 of that year. My mother had been placed in a nursing home in November of 2000 and was doing poorly. She was ninety four and had a blockage in her descending aorta. It was a matter of time before she would pass on. She died on February 13, 2001 and I spent my workshop weekend dialoguing and journaling on my lifelong relationship with her. What follows is an excerpt from that journal section called the Meaning Dimension, process meditation, section – Peaks, Depths and Explorations in which I identify my best and worst experiences[102]:

"2/18/2001 Death comes up in the dream extensions (of this journal). I had a dream of mother in a tent along with other souls who were milling around on a wide plain in purgatory. I was trying to find her but did not succeed. It was evident that it was a different world because the Sun shifted in the sky to a lower point, it actually jumped lower in the sky. The death journey started with mother's death and remains a mystery...(dreamt in 2000.)

Themes – Focusing on Death = Developing feelings associated with the devouring chasm, never ending feelings of sorrow and pain, disconnectedness at death. Yet a whole new world was happening with a shift of the sun in the sky. It was the end of an era, as Mother would say."

That was a difficult time for me because I had lived two separate lives: Mother always wanted me to be conventional and follow the path she understood, but I was destined to follow a circuitous path toward being authentic that continued to include psychological astrology. Mother's death symbolized release from that conflict on one level: following the status quo which is conservative thinking vs. following my own path giving expression to psychological astrology. Journaling was a way to bridge the gaps between these two worlds. That is why journaling was so important to me. I had been journaling for 40 years. Opening the doors to my unconscious through dreams was a daily task for me. The insights I gleaned from these dreams showed emotional pain, but hope too because of dreams like the following:

"I was on a raging river in a small motor boat. I was riding the waves. Then I came to a tributary and drifted on it through tepid waters in which trees with branches full of bugs drooped over so their branches touched the water. It was so thick I could hardly move the branches out of my eyes. As I continued through this tributary, I could see a faint light far ahead in a clearing where the river widened. I followed toward that light."

This clearly represents the diversions of my life going through the entanglements on the surface of water, the bridge between conscious and unconscious. I follow the light of illumination but it is barely visible and at the great distance. I am dealing with long term goals.

Now, because my dreams were so helpful in guiding my life and giving me hope, I want to give instruction to the reader on how to remember dreams, record them and work with them. The first instruction is to sleep without an alarm clock and do not hastily arise in the morning. But lie there and go back into a reverie, being open to the images of the dream life upon awakening and do not move. Keep a notebook with 2 sections: Daily log, and Dream enlargement sections. Answer these questions when you have sufficiently begun to collect images of the night's dreaming. Write the dream content immediately and later in the day reflect on the day. The directions in Figure 1 may be helpful, based on those in Ira Progoff's *At a Journal Workshop.*[103]

I also refer the reader to Jungian Dream Analysis methods as explicated in Ira Progoff's *Intensive Journal Workbook*, Dialogue House Associates, Inc. 80 East 11th Street - Suite 305, New York, New York, 10003-6008.

On awakening, write in your daily log:

How did you feel upon awakening?

Write down the dream images as they occur.

Give the dream a name but save for later the full detail in your dream enlargement section. Each dream has a beginning, an action section and an ending.

During the day or at end of day

Record the day's events and the movement of your emotions.

At the end of your day,

Record your thoughts and feelings related to the day

Reread the dream of today. Close your eyes breathe deeply and go to the dream enlargement section. Wait. In your mind re-enter the dream of the day and continue to be aware of images, feelings and actions in the dream. Now on the screen of the mind's eye guide the development of the dream. You do not restrict or direct this process. Record associations with people, places and things in our life – the dream extension.

Stop and reread what you have written so far. Become aware of the feelings and emotions in you as those experiences were taking place.

Consider some key questions: What was the atmosphere and tone that accompanied the dream? What awareness is kindled in you? Is the dream communicating a message to you? Do you perceive hints and indicators as you read it back?

Have a dialogue with a character in your dream; between your dream ego and a character. This is called active the imagination technique. See Robert Johnson, *Inner Work*.

With a recurrent distressing or traumatic dream, relax and imagine a different ending to the dream and write it down.

Figure 1. Dream Processing Instructions

VII. Types or Categories of Dreams/Fantasies

A. Precognitive Dreams

Dreams can be pre-cognitive. Although speaking in symbols, it is sometimes difficult to discern the exact prediction, until months or years later.

Abraham Lincoln dreamed he foresaw his own death, as reported by his biographer Lamon who noted the following from Lincoln's diary:

"About ten days ago, I retired very late. I had been up waiting for important dispatches from the front. I could not have been long in bed when I fell into a slumber, for I was weary. I soon began to dream. There seemed to be a death-like stillness about me. Then I heard subdued sobs, as if a number of people were weeping. I thought I left my bed and wandered downstairs. There the same pitiful sobbing broke the silence, but the mourners were invisible. I went from room to room; no living person was in sight, but the same mournful sounds of distress met me as I passed along. It was light in all the rooms; every object was familiar to me; but where were all the people who were grieving as if their hearts would break? I was puzzled and alarmed. What could be the meaning of all this? Determined to find the cause of a state of things so mysterious and so shocking. I kept on until I arrived at the East Room, which I entered. There I met with a sickening surprise. Before me was a catafalque, on which rested a corpse wrapped in funeral vestments. Around it were stationed soldiers who were acting as guards; and there was a throng of people, some gazing mournfully upon the corpse, whose face was covered, others weeping pitifully. 'Who is dead in the White House?' I demanded of one of the soldiers. 'The President', was his answer; 'he was killed by an assassin!' Then came a loud burst of grief from the crowd, which awoke me from my dream. I slept no more that night; and although it was only a dream, I have been strangely annoyed by it ever since."[104]

Consider the dream of the author, 11/30/1991:

"I was at a social work agency (the image in the dream looked like the hospital where I worked) and had clerical staff working for me. I gave an orientation to a new group of new students and new employees. Our offices were in a large room that had a number of desks. Very similar to a library at a college. There was a revolution. A group

headed by Dr. Medina (a psychiatrist) in a neighboring institution started a coup (actually looked like the Behavior health building on campus of the hospital where I worked). I was to deal with the transition of employees from their former workplaces to ours and give them orientation to their new jobs. I had a wooden spear that I held to show my authority as I helped them make this transition. As I was going down the stairs and the doorway, I stopped there holding the spear at the doorway waiting for the group of new employees to arrive. Outside was a group (6 or more) of employee-prisoners who had been freed. They were dressed in Robin Hood type clothes with red epaulettes with strings that hung over their shoulders. They were shooting arrows at the buildings, the hospital. A van soon came with these employees. I took them upstairs. They were old, emaciated and poor looking. I showed them upstairs to the library and had them sit down."

Facts came to light 14 years later. In 2005 as newly appointed Chief of Social Work in a Veterans Affairs (VA) Hospital where I had been working for 20 years, I was given the responsibility to increase our social work department from 7 to 20 then to 44 over the next 8 years. There was funding for new social work and therapist positions since the war in Iraq and Afghanistan occurred from 2003 and the VA was preparing for the onslaught of post-traumatic stress and other mental illness casualties from these wars. I was the Employee Assistance Coordinator and for years would orient new employees to their hospital jobs. With the federal money for new mental health programs, I was involved as a gatekeeper in interviews and orientation of many new employees to our departments of mental health and social work. Thus, I was kind of a sentry as the dream dramatizes bringing people into new government jobs. With the advent of new employees from 2005 to 2013, they joined the departments in social work and mental health. The dream portrays social workers as Robin Hood types; which is a really funny analogy as these people came from the private sector, many to better paying jobs with the Federal government which was funded by taxes (robbing from the rich to give to the poor). Dr. Rodolfo Medina came on board to our hospital as Chief of Mental Health in 2005. We became fast friends and collaborated to join social work and mental health departments called the Behavioral Sciences Department. This was a model used by other hospitals in our system but when we presented our case to administration, they refused it. We were creating a coup and 'slinging arrows' at their long held beliefs that the two departments should be kept separate. Furthermore, Dr. Medina was to be the Clinical Director and I was to be the Administrative Director of the combined departments – another goal administration was against. So we tried to revolutionize the organization of the hospital but used primitive weapons (bows and arrows in the dream) and therefore the coup had no effect and failed.

The astrological facts of the timing of the dream (represented as a failed revolution) is borne out by the aspects of the radix chart Age Point (which shows developmental potential or none) opposed to my Sun (true purpose or will); the nodal Age Point (which represents the shadow and desire) was square my natal Uranus (revolution) on that date. In other words, the dream was showing me that the combining of the departments and the revolution would be energized, but not the outcome because it was not aligned with my destiny and was opposed to my karmic duty.[105]

B. Teleological-healing Dreams

Dreams can have a healing message leading one to resolve neurotic conflicts and fears shifting consciousness to embrace a renewal of faith and confidence. As any longitudinal study of dreams over many years, the symbols and the dreamer's relation to them can change in effecting moods and attitudes as the dreams work out their dramas toward resolution.

I had threatening water dreams in the decade of the 1970's when I first started recording and interpreting my own dreams. I was in my 20's and trying to identify with a career. But I was ambivalent about it because I was not truly invested in what jobs were available in the market. I had been filled with a sense of anxiety, a sense of foreboding at the meaning of these dreams because I had a series of water dreams: tidal waves would rush into a town and knock down the buildings on the shore as if they were stick houses. This was followed by another fearful dream at a later time:

> *I was in a building and had the water seep into the foundation and slowly fill up the house threatening to drown me; a later dream of having a wave, the crest of which was about to break over me, plummet droplets of water from its height hitting my shoulders and head. It woke me up in a sense of terror.*

At this stage of my life, I had been in "incubation" with my occupational ego identity. Eric Erickson called it a developmental stage in young adulthood, a "moratorium" on life as the process of identity formation in the psyche was beginning to give one's life direction in the world of work.[106] All through my early and middle twenties, I had put off reconciling myself to a career path. Developmentally, I had been unconscious of and passive-aggressive in reaction to what I perceived to be social pressure coming from what I thought was other people trying to control my path in life. My water dreams were threatening me to get going, to get moving from this undifferentiated student identity to a more assertive goal-oriented ego identity or be overcome by oceanic obscurity and stagnation.

The Jungian analyst James Hall put my dreams into context in the following:

"Physical danger to the dream ego is not dangerous to the waking ego … the most common endings to such dreams is for the dream ego to 'surface' into the waking ego-identity during the (wave) threat. The shift of the dream ego to the waking ego is a frequent lyses (ending). It is important to look beyond the mere presence of physical danger to the dream ego and make some assessment of its meaning within a dream, which will vary depending on the context."[107]

The meaning was that I needed to become assertive with my energies in determining a life path. The very effort of doing so meant I had to stand on my own and not be nurtured anymore by the water of life – the passive student lifestyle.

In my horoscope the planet Neptune (delusion, the sea and water) is opposed the Moon (sense of belonging, the anima),[108] so there was a delusion that I had to remain passive and unformed to have a sense of belonging to my family; as a perpetual student I would just drift along on the waters of life.

My youth had been a moratorium on life by my going to college, graduate school and spending two years in the Peace Corps in which I had been avoiding finding a career path. The dreams would continue to be threatening for years until I resolved this issue.

But then I had a transformative dream as I was considering a focusing on counseling as a career:

I was overcome by a wave and went under the water. Rolling and twisting and turning through the surf, I was surprised that I could breathe underwater!

That image of breathing underwater is the same that came from a Doors group song in the 60's called "Yes the River Knows". The lyrics are:

Please believe me the River told me
Very softly wants you to hold me ooo
Free fall, flow River flows on and on it goes
Breathe underwater till the end,
Yes, the River knows…[109]

I have always been grateful to that dream of breathing underwater symbolizing a miracle, a magical Uranian reversal of the laws of nature. It represented a turning point at that stage of my young adult life. In the sense that, no matter how fearful I was of standing on my own, I would be able to breathe – even defying the natural elements turned against me and living on. Hall goes to add:

> *"Disaster dreams point rather to a potentially abrupt and possibly violent change in the tacit background of the ego image that has dominated consciousness. They indicate the potentiality of a major shift in ego-image structure. Such changes, if therapeutically contained, can be transformative."*[10]

My dream life with water themes since that time have no longer had the same type of terrifying water threatening to destroy me. I became comfortable in my own skin. At the same time in my life, I had found a way to specialize and focus my energy on life with renewed vigor and purpose that actually led to my going into psychiatric social work. What is more, I found that the reveries of my childhood and early development brought me to memories of a story I had loved as a child, The tale and its development followed my cathartic dream – it is about a child who is a chimney sweep, goes underwater, drowns and is reborn into manhood as a great man of science.[111] The concept of death and rebirth or redemption is the point of the story and is what I identified with.

From that time on I had dreams of turning water into ice, hovering above water, scuba diving and traveling down a deep river gorge happily sailing along with the current, not desperately trying to avoid the water overcoming me.

The autobiographical context of the following water dream was that my supervisor removed me from a job as psychiatric therapist in an outpatient clinic in 1990. I thought he removed me because I had threatened him with my newfound professional autonomy as a psychotherapist. An autonomy that I had found with difficulty and which I would not give up easily. The dream, nonetheless, shows a new flexibility with my autonomy as a therapist and the reversal of a possible threat to a new attitude in the following:

> *12/21/1991 I was on a boat ride. A man and his wife were on it too. They were too straight-laced. She had short 50's type hairdo and he had those wire rims on the bottoms with plastic on top. He steered the boat in a circle. I told him to go slower as he was going too fast. After that he went round and round. I found out he had been in the Navy for 20 years. He was pilot on a ship. Now he was retiring.*

(My supervisor was a retired Marine from combat who actually later retired from active life. I was relieved that he was at the helm.)

In the following dream, I am trying to get back to psychiatric social work and had to 'cross the water' or find renewal of my commitment to that goal. There seemed to be obstacles to my finding my own way but I found solutions:

2/27/1992 I was walking, traveling along a shore and there were some men fishing in shallow waters beside it. I had my destination far off in the distance and needed to go through the waters where the men were fishing to get there. I asked them if I could cross through their waters. No answer. They ignored me. Instead I went starting to go across the water at a place where I did not need their permission but had to expend effort on my own by climbing a cliff. It was full of precipices and I could hardly maneuver. Yet the shoreline of the other side was in view and that was my destination.

1/26/93 I was levitating a few feet above a river being pushed by the wind along a shoreline. It blew me where it might and I was aware of the purpose and intelligence behind it. It took me out to the middle of the river. I hovered over the water there but did not fall in. I thought I would.

These dreams reflect a new commitment to my life goal as a therapist and mastery in dealing with the element of my identity and the unknown. I had started my private practice and began to feel a sense of accomplishment. So I found an outlet for my specialist's role as a psychotherapist in addition to working in the hospital where I was deployed to where the administration wanted me to be.

5/ 28/94 I was swimming in this beautiful yet swift moving river. It was invigorating and full of beautiful vegetation on the sides. Yet there was an aspect of danger. I saw an old man with a beard swimming too. It's one of the best things to do – swim the river.

Below the circuitous path of trying to find my way as a psychiatric social worker. I had actually tried private practice but I had my fears. I decided to try my own psychotherapy business in spite of these fears and the dangers:

5/1/95 I was in the water. A group of kids were having fun on a boat. It was at the Huntingdon (hometown) swimming pool. Suddenly I was pushed under the water and could not breathe. I woke up. Now I was breathing air, no longer yearning for the womb or a collective state of belonging. But I was threatened by a return to that state because I wanted to be a man on my own.

11/20/95 I was at this hotel. I impulsively went to the pool for a swim. Was going to go off the diving board but there was an obstruction so I went off the side and dove really deep to the point I almost could not keep my breath. I came up to the surface and the thrill of it was fun.

Having begun to master the art of psychotherapy, I had the feeling of being fulfilled in a thriving practice. I had renewed faith in my confidence. Actually at this time I also went back to providing psychotherapy at the hospital where I also worked.

9/10/2000 I left this large group of people with a man. Walked across a meadow until we came to a river. We had to cross. He pointed his finger and changed the water into ice. I was skeptical saying that I could not believe he could do this because downstream all the heat accumulated from fireplaces would prevent it but here was not the case.

This dream represented a transitional state in which I foresaw my real mother's death as a transformation of elements (from earth to air-spirit); and I was instructed and led by my spirit guide.

3/12/03 I was on a river. Was with my family who could not come with me to board a boat on the river. I tried to board it but was swept underwater by the current. I knew it would take me downstream. I saw myself emerging from the water, standing, wet with my wallet; seeking respite in a hotel where I could stay to rest after my ordeal. Somehow I was facing a challenge and my psyche was preparing me for the next chapter of my life in which I would have to stand alone.

2/29/04 Dream of a tidal wave coming from a distance. I was watching it come. I was not running from it as much as I was wary of it. Somehow it passed me by or petered out before it got to me. The unknown is not threatening to me at this time but I am seeing impersonal forces destroying mankind – natural disasters. There are also concurrent incidents of increasing real tidal waves worldwide due to global warming.

9/10/09 I was seeing water on the streets. Saw a scarfed woman with her body lying in the water. I swam to a deeper part where the waves were swirling. There were two unknown women in the water but we were smiling. We swam across the river, no problem. We landed on a beach where there were marines who had amphibious boats on the shore.

Now my psyche is preparing me for a new chapter in my life. The new shores represented the collective life of the group where I was accompanied by soldiers much the way I am at my work in a Veterans'

Hospital. The objective connection with collective consciousness was becoming more acceptable and agreeable. This represents a disciplined and yet chaotic stage of my interaction with the outside world but was also exciting.

C. Dreams reveal a personal unconscious structure

Dreams can show the dreamer another side of conscious life in an event or in relation to a person that we are not aware of. *"The shadow is an unconscious part of the personality characterized by traits and attitudes, whether negative or positive, which the conscious ego tends to reject or ignore. Persons of the same sex as the dreamer personify it in dreams. Consciously assimilating one's shadow usually results in an increase in energy."*[12] The repression of the shadow can be liberated by not embracing one duality or the other ego image but by giving conscious expression to both.

> *"The shadow is simply an alter-ego image personifying those contents that have not been assigned to the conscious personality. If the shadow projection is indeed an integral part of one's character structure, dreams often show the dream-ego engaged in shadow activity or attitude."*[13]

The shadow mediates the personal unconscious with the conscious ego. When we are unaware of the shadow, then we project on others these negative traits we have within ourselves. The inferior, less developed and immature part of our ego is sinister, manipulative and power hungry. But the shadow is not just an evil structure in the psyche, it can express itself as hidden motives, desires, and efforts that we act on to dominate others. If we ignore these ego needs altogether, we are living only half a life. Yet to express these needs without reflection can have regrettable consequences. We are all aware of how we can label a person negatively when we are just projecting our own negative feelings or attributes onto them.

When one is aware of one's own shadow, the shadow can introduce moral problems confronting us, and lend a power and depth to the personality that is missing from those who see their egos as only good. The good and evil aspects of the ego complex are both needed against the exigencies of the external world. The interplay between our "dark and light sides" of the ego when consciously applied in relationships can bring a balance to our conscious attitude, strengthening our resolve and will.

In astrological psychology, the shadow is related to what Bruno Huber calls the Moon Node Horoscope. It is a dimension of the personal unconscious. *"The Moon Node Horoscope touches among* other things, on the subject of the shadow… as part of the psyche which holds drives, wishes and projections that are inaccessible to everyday consciousness".[114]

When I had the following dream over 30 years ago, it seemed the character was alien to me. But since I knew about Jung's shadow structure in the psyche, I started to *own* the personality traits of the main character. Instead of projecting them onto another, I discovered a side of myself that I did not want to face or recognize, my shadow. It took some time and reflection for me to realize the main character or dream ego was my shadow. I called him Fagin.

Dream on 07/12/1992 – Fagin was with this poverty stricken family but they ate well. The food was mixed with rice and meat. They ate on metal plates but the stew meat dish was made of dog meat. The man was tall, lanky and a dirty man. He had a woman who worked for him, a servant type but who was from a higher class. She added discipline and daintiness to his world. But she was addicted to a white powder. She would spill quantities on the table and pick it up with her finger and eat it. It was a narcotic. The man loved her secretly. One time she was tidying a room and the door was closed. A shadow appeared under the crack in the door. It was he peering at her. He entered and clumsily embraced her, hardly touched her, telling her in his drawl, his affections for her.

The Author's Drawing of Fagin

This man had gained the trust of 2 bearded schoolmasters, but in the process had stolen their books. They caught on and went to his house to assemble the contraband where they found over 3,000 volumes of 3 varieties of books he had stolen over the years. He had gained their confidence and had betrayed them. Before this discovery, they were about to bestow upon him the assistant principal of the school job.

I was walking with this man. He was very friendly on the surface but was a sleazy person – a snake. I confronted him with all this garbage he had hidden in this one corridor. It was rotten. He poked me slightly in the ribs and smiled saying he never did like me. He was despicable in his cowardice trying to pretend he was assertive when he was not. I had just uncovered another of his games and he was trying to weasel out.

In this dream, part of me is the man pictured here. I am poor, and feed my family dog meat. I have depraved tastes in women. I am untrustworthy and a thief. In spite of being given honors, I am unworthy. I secretly pollute the earth with my garbage. In the end, I am dishonored.

As a psychotherapist I had dealt with women primarily who were dependent types, sometimes addicted to narcotics or other drugs. I had to keep ethically removed from personal relations with them, keeping my professional boundaries and the treatment process was strictly confidential. I had studied the Jungian psychoanalytic model and incorporated it into my practice over the years. Although I did not receive formal training in Jungian analysis, I was empirically grounded as a Jungian. I felt confident as I professionally confronted issues with clients (like their own shadows and anima-animus), concepts that were foreign to them.

The shadow is not an intellectual concept. It is a living symbol reminding us of the duality of our natures. Most lay people discount symbols of the dreaming psyche and don't seriously study them. In addition, to ascribe negative traits of the shadow to themselves seems masochistic and doomed to futility. In my relationship with clients, they resisted this interpretation because they thought counseling has a purpose to only rid them of suffering. Actually symptoms have a different meaning for the Jungians. Symptoms are not only to be reduced, they are to be understood in their full meaning through the in the life story of the individual.

How does one assimilate the shadow? In a letter C.G. Jung wrote to a patient, it gives a clue as to the process of owning the unlovable part of yourself.[115]

"There can be no resolution, only patient endurance of the opposites which ultimately spring from your own nature. You, yourself are a conflict that rages in itself and against itself, in order to meet its incompatible substance... we are crucified between opposites and delivered up to the torture until the reconciling third takes shape. Do not doubt the rightness of the two sides within you; let whatever may happen, happen. The apparently unendurable conflict is proof of the rightness of your life. A life without inner contradiction is either only half a life or else a life in the Beyond, which is destined only for angels. But God loves human beings more than angels"

In another compendium of Jung's letters he goes on to say[116]

"It is a very difficult and important question, what you call the technique of dealing with the shadow. There is, as a matter of fact, no technique at all, inasmuch as technique means that there is a known and perhaps even a prescribable way to deal with a certain difficulty, or task. It is rather a dealing comparable to diplomacy or statesmanship. There is, for instance, no particular technique that would help us to reconcile two political parties opposing each other... If one can speak of a technique at all, it consists solely in an attitude. First of all, one has to accept and to take seriously into account the existence of the shadow. Secondly, it is necessary to be informed about its qualities and intentions. Thirdly, long and difficult negotiations will be unavoidable... Nobody can know what the final outcome of such negotiations will be. One only knows that through careful collaboration the problem itself becomes changed. Very often certain apparently impossible intentions of the shadow are mere threats due to unwillingness on the part of the ego to enter upon a serious consideration of the shadow. Such threats diminish usually when one meets them seriously."

A useful technique to engage the shadow is found in Robert A. Johnson's *Inner Work: Using Dreams and Active Imagination for Personal Growth*. Using a dialogue with the shadow and the ego, one can expand one's understanding of this autonomous complex in one's life journey.[117]

Bruno Huber goes on to explain how the Moon Node Horoscope symbolizes *"a mirror sphere in which our motivations, wishes and deeds are projected by certain incidents of the past (our karma) into our present."*[118] This represents the shadow in the Jungian sense.

I was dealing with these conflicts by interpreting my dreams; I discovered my traits that I was repressing. And the Moon Node Horoscope (MNH) interpretation put it in a context that could be explained as: the Moon of my MNH is in the first house putting feelers out for acceptance, the north node in the 5th is conjunct Venus in Sagittarius giving an over-impulsive and amorous nature. Sex, without having to relate to a partner but only seeing a person as a unit of pleasure, is a common male fantasy. The woman client in the dream is an anima projection. (Next page.)

It is worth pointing out that the interpretation of the shadow figure in dreams takes the form of a dialogue between the dreamer and the figure, whether it be shadow or anima personification. This dialogue is written as if the shadow or anima figures are autonomous figures. In this case, Fagin was to be addressed as he appeared in the dream and accepted for what he was. It is evident from Hillman's work that:[119]

"Personifications of our mature fate are figures of our fantasies and all things in the psyche which we do not produce, but which produce themselves, have their own life. "Know thyself in Jung's terms means to become familiar with, to open oneself to and listen to, that is, to know and discern, daimons."[120]

And in a dialogue that is how the daimon is set free as an accepted manifestation of our souls.

One has to get rid of prejudices in thinking if one is to engage in such activities as dialogue with the shadow. The first mistake is believing that authenticity is trying to be a consistent self-identity devoid of these parts – the shadow and anima. Rather, as Hillman points out:

"Authenticity is the perpetual dismemberment of being and not-being a self, a being that is always in many parts, like a dream with a full cast. We all have identity crises because a single identity is a delusion of the monotheistic mind that would defeat Dionysus at all costs... Authenticity is in the illusion, playing it, seeing through it from within as we play it, like an actor who sees through his mask and can only see in this way"

In the Huber Method, any planet can reflect an autonomous ego state when it is isolated, not all connected and integrated together by aspects. In analysis of the chart, one can see the lone planet that is apart from a grouping. That planet represents a part of ourselves that is disconnected and its archetypal energies act on their own, independently. This is true in the radix, in the house and in the nodal chart. That planet can represent our shadow too.

To ferret out all the inferior parts of our life experience in our life history from the nodal chart is one way of chronicling the shadow. We recognize that we are playing different roles, some of which are somewhat shameful, embarrassing. Even so, most of our shadow activity is unconscious because we tend not to "see the log in our eye but in our neighbor's eye"… through projection. But if one studies one's own life, one finds an autobiographical history. But this history has to rely on memory. However, this memory and *"historical reality is only a cover for soul significance, only a way of adapting the archetypal sense of mystery and importance to a consciousness engrossed in historical facts. If the image does not come as history, we may not take it as real."*[121]

We can appreciate the shadow as power, wish fulfillment and the unconscious drive's expression in my dream. However, the example of wanting to have sex with the woman who was a drug addict was representative of my anima, a secret wish which I could not consciously accept. I had fantasies about having anonymous sex with a woman who I had no responsibility to engage in the complications of a relationship. The shadow does want to engage in fantasies in the real world and will present them as compulsions in dreams.

D. Dreams of Anima and Saturn, Moon and Venus in the Radix, House and Moon Node Charts

The anima is a Jungian concept – a structure of the collective unconscious that can be revealed by analysis of dreams. (See Figure

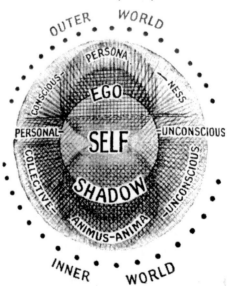

Figure 1. Structure of Consciousness
based on Jolande Jacobi's overview in *The Psychology of C. G. Jung*

1). The anima expression in the psyche of both sexes is erected on the experience of the child with the caretaker mother. The different experiences of a man or woman with the contrasexual unconscious complexes (anima and animus), is based on the original relationship with the mother and the self.

> *"For both sexes, the self as the center of the total psyche is experienced in immediate identity with the body. Thus, it (the self) takes on characteristics of the exterior physical self."*[122]

> *The boy experiences his original identity with the mother as a relation of like to unlike, as a relation to a non-self, to an 'other', an opposite, symbolized by all the obvious sexual differences... his self discovery takes place in opposition to the primary relationship with the mother and this effects greater isolation through its new emphasis on objectivity and ego consciousness."*[123]

In the examples of the feminine provided here, I will discuss how the stages of anima development in a man can effect his relationships with women and how he can project onto a woman either good or evil, depending on the maturity of his inner anima image.

In this section we shall also follow the development of the male consciousness and the anima as represented by archetypal planets and their symbolism and relationship in the horoscope.

First we shall deal with Saturn in the most primary relationship between mother and child; that undifferentiated stage of development where the mother is everything represented by the Great Mother. Next we shall deal with the Moon and the emerging male's need to relate beyond the mother to the opposite sex with sympathetic understanding. Finally we shall deal with the development of erotic love and differentiation of the anima in man from sex associated with the planet Venus. We shall define the anima and its development as follows:

> *"As the personality emerges from pure unconsciousness, the transformative character also becomes independent and is experienced as such. The transformative character drives toward development. Both positive and negative experiences of the elementary character of the anima are examples of the ambivalence that is typical of the Great Mother... The male experiences this aspect of the Feminine directly and indirectly as provocative, as a force that sets him in motion and impels him toward change... The anima or soul image which the male experiences in the female, is his own inner femininity and soulfulness, an element of his own psyche. But the anima as Jung pointed out from the very first is formed in part by the male's personal as well as*

archetypal experience of the Feminine. The man's anima figure, which has found its expression in myth and art of all times, is the product of genuine experience of the nature of the Feminine.[124]

This element of the unconscious, the anima, is found symbolically within the Huber Method with its 3 charts (radix, house and nodal); Saturn, Moon and Venus represent aspects of the anima.

Saturn's placement in the 3 charts can represent the Great Mother at her most basic level and its development through karmic influences (moon node chart), as illustrated in natural abilities (radix) and environmental influences (house chart). The Great Mother, represented by Saturn is depicted by Bruno and Louise Huber in *The Planets and their Psychological Meaning* as follows:

"In connection with the earth and matter, Saturn has been known as the Great Mother since time immemorial. We know from our own experience how feelings of well being and protection provided by the mother can make us feel good about ourselves. Saturn's maternal nature demands that everything is in order and all dangers and sources of disruption are eliminated. As a protective power, Saturn wants to be completely sure that everything runs smoothly. That is the minimal demand for the basic need for security. A mother constantly watches over her child so that it comes to no harm. She is always on call and sees to the vital necessities. For the child she is the life-preserving entity who provides everything, feeds, protects and guides. As the maternal function, Saturn brings up the child to be a responsible adult who is able to look after himself and control matter. Saturn's position in the horoscope reveals the influence of the mother and also the existential possibilities of the family."[125]

Beyond the experience of the Mother the male then learns to relate to others and puts out feelers to find sympathetic partners who will accept him. Relationships beyond the physical mother require an adaptation of anima development beyond the need for security. Bruno and Louise Huber identify the Moon as the basic probing aspect of the feeling person to tell if they are accepted or rejected by others. The need for nurturance, acceptance, and love comes from the Moon and its placement in the houses can determine if the person is ready to contact others and be loved unconditionally or if they feel others may expect conditions from them to return love[126]. The Moon represents another mutation of the anima complex.

Maureen Demot identifies psychological states of the Moon to be loving feelings, belonging, closeness, warmth and tenderness, vulnerability to rejection, dependency, and self protectiveness.[127]

These psychological states vary from person to person and determine whom they will choose as a lover.

Beyond the need for security, relatedness and feelings of being accepted by others the anima develops into another stage as the male matures. The planet Venus represents the erotic, seeker of sexual pleasure for Demot, and aesthetic love of beauty and she identifies psychological states of the Venus archetype as gratification on a sensual level. But Venus has a higher level of expression, that of partnership between equals which manifests in marriage of man and woman. This puts the sensual pleasure of Venus in the context of a known person associated with feelings of affection, justice and commitment.

Anima symbols of the Feminine are depicted in ancient cultures from preliterate times: Isis has elements of the terrible mother and good mother which is a projected form of the inward plane of the collective unconscious contents that are mirrored (onto a Goddess)[128]. The historical roots of the Feminine in man in ancient times takes the form of the Goddess presiding over matriarchal cultures. But since the Enlightenment, in the 1700's, where the male ego consciousness dominated science, religion and culture, the feminine anima archetypes were negatively relegated to the back waters of the 'devouring mother', the all consuming Mother who could not let her male child grow up. This archetype is much broader than just a negative influence; in the context of historical evolution, the Great Mother has many positive attributes.

We are giving an explication of the male's consciousness especially as it relates to the feminine within him – the anima. But this structure is unconscious, it is not perceived or known directly. At first one becomes aware of it only through dreams and fantasies.

> "As inward phenomena (anima figures) are not assigned to the outside world but they retain, as in the case of dreams, their character of projections. Thus these anima figures appear to the dream ego as something to deal with in the drama of the unfolding dream. As projections onto the outside world, the anima can invigorate, stimulate, instill creativity and erotize the male ego. The contents of these anima figures are de facto 'psychic contents' that are experienced by the dream ego in projection as outside contents."[129]

From the evidence of the play of the Great Mother archetype in the development of civilization, it is clear that the anima compels the man to action. As a female image in his dreams, the anima image compels the man to pass through stages of development.

It starts out with the real, biological mother, and then in relationships with the opposite sex, as an undifferentiated figure inciting sexual passion. But once it matures, the anima image develops and can lead the male ego to develop its own inner feminine identity, which reflects feelings of yearning, love, creativity, relatedness and redemption – all supporting a man's maturational development. At later stages, after midlife, the anima image can be a spiritual guide. The dream below demonstrates how the anima image of the dream is synchronized and timed with the movement of sensitive points in the horoscope, in this case with the Age Point conjunct natal Pluto in the 8th house. The dream gives a message that can impart faith in the guidance from a higher inner authority.

> *3/27/96 I was sitting with a group of men who were sitting cross legged in yoga positions. There were glassy eyed as if stoned but I did not see any drugs. Above them hovered in the air an Indian goddess, sitting in the lotus position. Her eyes were slightly off center and she did not touch the ground but stared passively at me. She had a headdress. As one is impelled by the anima to act, one's guide on a spiritual level can, in fact, be quite tangible as a Wise Woman guru and lead one to discoveries of enhanced consciousness.*

In the moon node chart Saturn represents the past karmic form of the Great Mother as an anima image. In the radix chart the Moon represents the loving need to relate to the personal mother or caretaker that sets the stage for good personal adjustment in relationships. A dose of eros as signified by Venus signifies the sexual passion that fires up the ego to a state of love leading hopefully to commitment. These tendencies are inherent in the personal unconscious of every male, transferring from the collective unconscious to the ego – making it come alive. The Great Mother, the Sexual Partner and Wife are universal and timeless symbols that go beyond our conception of the current or historical partners or personalities in our own life.

In my moon node chart, Saturn sits in the 8th house. The nodal chart represents karmic, inner resources, a gift from a former life, if you will. For me, it signifies the potential for rebirth on psychic and physical levels. Yoga and meditation represent such paths. To be led in a dream by a wise woman figure to a greater self-realization of peace created for me the faith in a guardian angel. Saturn is not aspected in my nodal chart and represents an objective approach to life, withdrawn from the exigencies of outer world involvement, with a capacity for detachment. As such it operates as an autonomous complex. In the practice of yoga, Saturn has both positive (peace and calm) qualities and relatively negative ones (withdrawal from the outer Western world).

In the house and radix charts Saturn is situated in my 9th house and represents a more developed spiritually conscious symbol of the anima or the feminine archetype. I have been practicing yoga since 1969 where I was taught the Hatha Yoga technique. Saturn in the 9th house compels me to the practice of yoga as a spiritual discipline and as a source of security. I propose that my "Angel" was working through my anima in the above dream, bringing me back to a spiritual discipline (as I had not been practicing regularly for 30 years). She guided me as a Saturn image, the feminine archetype, to be more responsible for my spiritual development. Since 2000, I have been practicing Hatha Yoga 5-6 days a week.

Saturn in the 9th house in the radix/house charts and the dream synchronistically predisposed me to living the experience of Hatha Yoga in my spiritual life (9th house represents change in consciousness and spirituality). To me yoga practice centers me on my body and gives me peace by going inward in a busy outer world experience. I practice it 20 minutes a day and find the inward calming influence vital to my sense of security.

The Moon in my radix chart is in the 4th 'family' house, opposite Neptune in the 10th 'career' house. The radix sets the stage for attitudes that condition a person to deal with areas of life. Thus my need for belonging was fulfilled in the home but I was continually deceived, confused and felt sensitive to rejection by the outer world all my life. This led to avoidance of career advancement and, as indicated in the chapter on water dreams, delayed my ego identification with an occupation. My anima guided me through love of a partner, and through my relationship with my wife gave me the focus to start a family and live out my role as a psychotherapist. My career goals were secondary and incidental to this main goal.

Venus in my 1st house and opposite Uranus had led me to sexual experiences with girls at an early age. The challenge for me was to learn to distinguish between sexual passion and commitment with one partner. I came back from two years abroad and got married to a wonderful individual. As I grow older the appreciation I have for my wife as my partner makes my love for her grow beyond physical love. She is my teacher, friend and guru in spiritual matters.

To be in contact with the symbols of the anima in the feminine archetype as symbolized in the dream and represented by Saturn and Moon in the radix chart can lead one to realize one's spiritual guides, as well as providing direction for anima development.

The feminine has positive attributes in the form of Saturn and the Moon's protective functions but also negative traits; for example, the

72

Plate 1
Artemis of Ephesus

possessive boundaries around the child as defined by the mother can be too rigid thus preventing her child from gaining independence and his/her own identity. Dependencies and extreme avoidant behavior can result from over controlling and manipulative nurturance.

Prehistory records the Great Goddess as having animal and human attributes. This is because of the state of consciousness of early man projected the synthesis of the nurturer with the "beast tamer."[130] Consider Artemis (Diana) at Ephesus in Turkey: a Goddess with bats, and other creatures hanging on to her dress but also a myriad of breasts to nurture her children (Plate 1). She was the incarnation of Goddess as Mother.

The Goddesses of old played the role of taming the male ego through the exclusion of males from the female blood rituals: menstruation, birthing and breast feeding (changing blood to milk); which were reserved exclusively for women. Men had to tame their libido, aggression and need for companionship during these rituals.[131] So as Great Mother figures, women and their rituals had civilizing roles to play as societies became more differentiated. They served to restrict and modify the male's expansive, object-related ego nature when stimulated by his libido.

The feminine also plays the role of seductress, as man projects his own desires onto her form. She therefore can weave a web of sexual magic that plummets the man's ego

Plate 2
Burney Relief, British Museum

into voluptuousness and lust. She appears to tempt men: the Harpies, Sirens, Mermaids contribute to this aspect of the feminine that leads men to dissolve their ego into voracious impulses of desire and fornication. (Plate 2). What man does to himself through unconscious identification with the feminine seductress in his own psyche is the subject of many love tragedies. Homer's Odyssey has Sirens luring men by their beautiful singing to crash on the rocks. The myth of Oedipus has this male killing his father and marrying his mother. The Marquis de Sade demonstrates the debauchery of the aristocracy at the time of the French revolution leading to his death.

The feminine archetype is also constellated into Terrible Mother of Death (Plate 3). She demands sacrifice of freedom and can devour the son by restriction, rejection and dissolution.

Then she loses her function as preserver and "keeper of the threshold."[132]

In this way the negative anima is expressed: by threats of exerting negative consequences on children who are dependent on her. Through her rejection, she can bring about death of those who she had brought to life and preserved through her care. The following dream reflects how I projected this quality onto my biological mother:

Plate 3
Coatlicue, Aztec Goddess of
Life and Death

June 1973: "Standing on the edge of a cliff with Mother on my back; I could not jump a chasm and reach the other side with her on my back. I put Mother down and jumped to the other side myself".

This dream occurred right before my joining the Peace Corps and going abroad for 2 years. Astrologically speaking, I was compelled to journey as a hero. To leave home and strike out on my own. The Age Point had moved to conjunct my North Node in the 5th house of my radix chart. The correspondence of this aspect and this action spurred me to create my own destiny.

Now that I have explored the role of the anima in the male psyche as manifested in his relationship with his own unconscious, I shall now turn to the animus in the female psyche and how this complex motivates her relationships with the opposite sex and can bring fulfillment or difficulty.

E. The Animus can reveal the man she will find and lead to individuation

The animus is a structure deep within the collective unconscious of the psyche (see Figure 1) of a woman. Before the child develops an ego, she identifies with the mother and has an affinity to the mother's unconscious thoughts, feelings and affects stemming from her instincts. Because the girl is the same sex as the mother, she does not have to develop an ego consciousness that defines herself as separate from the mother. Since the ego, as a structure of differentiation, is in a contra-position to the animus in the girl, there is less emphasis on developing an ego position with which to oppose the unconscious as compared to a boy. Instead, a girl's ego development takes place not in opposition to but in relation to her unconscious. She feels dependent on it and turns towards unconscious processes, not away from them.[133] For the girl, the mother-child relationship is one of identification, that mode of relating is stronger in women than in men. Her instinctive way of relating is through identification, not through discrimination; it leads to tendencies to become over-involved, overemotional, and to find and enmesh herself continually in the same situations.[134]

As the end stage of maturation of the animus exemplifies, the development of healthy relationships with men depends on whether the woman's ego psychologically manages her animus images to achieve greater wholeness and integrity of her personality. On the other hand if her ego is completely overwhelmed by the animus images she projects on a man, she becomes fixated at the stage where she is spellbound to follow/repel the animus images coming to her from her unconscious and falls for the projections of her own animus images. For example, Lara in the novel Dr. Zhivago by Boris Pasternak, has an animus that is totally buffaloed by the wealthy and immoral lawyer, Komarovsky. Lara becomes passive in Komarovsky's hands and cannot ward off his sexual advances, even though she has values which certainly oppose his. She feels so helpless at his advances that at one point she shoots him to keep him at bay.

At stage one of animus development, according to Ulanov, the girl's ego is totally enmeshed in identification with the mother. At stage two, the patriarchal stage, the ego of the girl is confronted with the male image which has numinous qualities and is alien to her. The girl understands at this stage with her heart not her head, and sees the male as a robber or penetrator who overpowers her sense of balance, overwhelms her consciousness and transforms her personality. If she becomes fixated, she becomes her 'father's daughter', creating a bondage to her animus with the idealized paternal preferences taking priority over her own ego needs. If she is unable to manage the masculine or animus image within herself, she can become crippled in assertiveness and be unable to defend herself against the world of consciousness and discrimination.[135]

She can become, as Ulanov describes the fixation, the anima woman.[136] She then becomes a victim of her own unconscious effect on men; she becomes for men whatever their anima projections demand of her, wish for or hope for. This results in her selling herself out, living a false identity, and harboring ego alienation towards men in some form.

Ulanov explains further… *"(she has) no ego position now… where personal preferences and points of view should be expressed, there is a vacuum instead; she expresses herself in vagueness, ambiguity and ambivalence".*[137] This leads ultimately to her being an appendage of her male partner, and she can have difficulty with her own aggressive feelings toward the males in her life. Power differences between herself and her partners are submitted to, as a result she can become depressed. She may be bound to a patriarchal partner who confines her to female roles and ideals that she happily conforms to at the expense of her ego. Thus she is overcome by the animus. This can result in a compensation where she becomes secretly manipulative, a vixen who knows men and what they want but uses their anima wishes and projections for her own ends – for power, status, and or material gain.

The animus has been associated with a collective unconscious complex in female psychology according C.G. Jung's psychoanalytic model.[138] In the description given above of the fixated anima woman, the content of the collective unconscious within her inflates her ego with grandiose plots and schemes which correspond to mythological figures of the witch, the harpie and the siren. The woman manipulates man into her lair of sexuality, only to cut him off from his independence and his masculine consciousness to suit her own ends. The situation ends in tragedy for both.

In a woman, the ego is not as differentiated as a conscious complex as in a man, although it mediates with the center of her psyche, the Self. When her ego is wedded, fixated and identified with her unconscious, it can have a powerful effect in receiving anima impressions from a man and reflecting them back to him as if she possesses the very traits the man were looking for in a woman. She can appear passive, childlike and powerless, given over to all a man's desires. But it is her subliminal cunning in identifying with the projected anima qualities from a man that can make her realize that she can actualize her fantasies for power, truth and justice and betray her coquettish appearance. When she is known better, the negative sphere of relationships comes out; her animus can be cold, non-personal and take a general nature of critical remarks made to others with whom the person is emotionally close.[139] The animus can subvert the intentions of the male ego and undermine relationships by its subtle emotional distancing. Although there is healthy animus development, it is not the concern of this work.

Here I am concerned with the problems associated with animus development as they relate to dreams and psychological astrology.

In astrological psychology the Sun is symbolic of the mental ego, which is a partly conscious structure that mediates between the inner world and reality.[140] 'Harsh' angular relationships (oppositions and squares) between the Sun and Pluto/Mars in a woman's horoscope can give hints to challenges to her confidence in self assertion necessary for animus development. In relationships with men, the animus becomes fixated when she cannot stand up against the strong male conscious focus with her own values intact.

The Sun in the radix represents *"a consciousness in which we stick to our own thoughts, convictions and opinions... The thinking self therefore has the power to discriminate, judge, react clearly and lucidly to the world with greater self-confidence, as a real I-entity taking full responsibility for its actions."*[141]

The animus can interact with the ego or Sun consciousness in negative ways and thus create conflicts in relationships. The Sun's aspects, its sign and position in the woman's radix chart can give hints to the way in which the animus can contaminate the ego without her being able to stop it.

In a woman's radix chart the Sun also represents her relationship with her father. In a female's life the father represents the first male she has an intimate relationship with while growing up. The archetype of the father is reflected in many possible manifestations of the real father: a father who is invisible, disengaged, involved, dependent, an authority, a monster, hero or warrior.

"The Sun's position provides useful psychological information about the father. It shows how we live the masculine paternal principle and can realize it with ourselves... The Sun's position usually tells us something about our real father. If weak we too lack self confidence and are afraid to assert ourselves and frequently suffer from low self esteem."[142]

Thus, aspects, position and sign of the Sun in the female's chart can represent not only how she relates unconsciously to her biological father, but also how her ego, self awareness and self confidence manifest in male relationships.

Most psychotherapies are designed to build a healthy 'executive function' of the ego through cognitive strategies.[143] The ego then is perceived as the center of the psyche with the ultimate say in the everyday functioning of life. What is our concern here, however, are the unconscious determinants at play in the psyche that create attitudes that reveal self defeating behavior patterns that interfere with development and self realization. These unconscious attitudes can be revealed by analyzing the position of the Sun in the radix, its aspects and sign.

In the course of child development, the female's relationship with her father is introjected or internalized and predisposes her to react/relate a certain way with male friends, co-workers, etc. Early psychoanalysts in the 1900's were somewhat limited in seeing women as independent agents with careers and autonomy. As Jung believed *"In women Eros is an expression of their true nature – the need to create and relate. (As she uses Logos) she gives rise to misunderstandings and annoying interpretations in the family circle and among friends. The animus consists of opinions instead of reflections or assumptions that lay claim to absolute truth."*[144] In spite of these limitations, the concepts of the animus and the Sun in the radix, are relevant to and associated with female autonomy and creation of psychic predispositions or attitudes toward men. Thus, an ever-evolving inner image from this paternal introject is morphed into unconscious attitudes and assumptions about the opposite sex.

This inner image of the male inside the feminine psyche creates a changing symbol that can develop throughout the life cycle. During the teenage years, it can be projected as "love" of the hero, the warrior, the muscle man – tall, dark and handsome, emphasizing physical characteristics. As a the female matures so can her inner image of the animus 'love' the magician, the professor, the spiritual guru, the master.[145] As she develops with the help of a more positive (house chart) experience and insight into her projections, she can learn to manifest these images as her masculine side – the animus. Many spiritual guides are females with well-developed egos and an awareness of their animus projections. They can transcend their assumptions of males and own their animus as part of their relational identities. But in cases where the animus possesses their hosts with negative assumptions, they tend toward destructive patterns in their life.

Animus possessions are called autonomous complexes that are in part identity and relational structures in the psyche.[146] We can imagine a mental state in which a woman is calculating – her thinking, filled with malice and intrigue that gets her into a state that she even wishes the death of others to achieve her own ends. Thus, she becomes her inner image, externalized. This process is unconscious and she does not realize that the male opponents she perceives have been created out of her own unawareness.

Sometimes if negative male experiences traumatize a young girl, this inner animus image can transform into a robber, thief or monster that is projected into an outward hatred of men.

Consider the case study Cynthia Burbank (fictitious name) who had a negative animus possession. Cynthia had a difficult childhood full of traumas. The sudden death of her mother (Saturn on her ascendant square Aquarian moon) created an inner child experience that lost her awareness of protection from the nurturer and resulted in her feeling unworthy. She was controlled by an overburdened father (Pluto square Saturn in the first house square the Moon in the third house) who she witnessed beating her sister. Cynthia's experiences with her father created a psychic predisposition toward men in which she was dependent on a father who was abusive. She developed a negative animus, and thus felt she had to keep a partner who treated her badly. Cynthia's unconscious attitude manifested in a *"Bluebeard, who secretly kills all his wives in a hidden chamber. In this form the animus personifies all the semiconscious, cold, destructive reflections about men that invade a woman in the small hours, especially when she has failed to realize some obligation of feeling."[147]* This image was projected outward on her actual husband who "robbed" her many times. Cynthia's animus was bound with a man who was a criminal, who raped her and who beat her in a blind fury whenever the mood struck him. Her psychological set up and life experience attracted people, situations and events that continued to poison her relationship with men. She carried assumptions and opinions that all men were cruel, stupid and mean. But what was really happening was a self-fulfilling prophesy buried deep in the psyche, an animus projection.

What we want to show with the case of Cynthia is how a negative animus father-image which was reflected in her unaspected Sun in her radix horoscope, compelled her to create a life pattern of imprisonment. And how eventually, through therapy, her life was turned around.

Cynthia's Sun was unaspected in the Low Point of the 2nd house. Cynthia's Sun, *"act(ed) independently and often unconsciously... and (was) not integrated into her chart as a whole and therefore, not a fully integrated part of the personality*"[148]. It was a radix chart with many challenges. Cynthia would project her negative inner male onto others and see them as controlling. With Saturn and Venus conjunct and square the Moon, she had an absence of love and protection and suppression of her ability to relate to men. So she was trapped. She was a victim of abuse and she had to fight her way out of power struggles with men to become a fully integrated being. Consequently, after a series of abusive events in her relationship with her husband, she eventually stabbed him with a pair of scissors. She ended up in jail. Thus these introjections of the male animus resulted in a self-fulfilling prophecy playing itself out in Cynthia's life. Her house chart shows little integration, with two disconnected linear aspect patterns.

Was she destined to live out such self-destructive patterns indefinitely? Her therapy with the late Maureen Demot, a Jungian astrologer, helped to turn her life around. In 2000, her Age Point was in the 8th house and opposed to her natal Sun. At that same time, transits of Saturn square Saturn, Pluto conjunction of Venus helped tear down her false beliefs about the powerlessness of her life. With Maureen Demot's guidance, the negative tape loops in her cognitive processing were resolved in psychotherapy and her inner animus image of the imprisoned male died away... she finally left her husband for good. This process was difficult for her; she had to take responsibility for creating her own reality. She eventually found that she had the potential to live a life that had no compulsions and she was free from the vortex of bad relationships.

Women experience the animus figures appearing in dreams as males, usually having to do with relationships. This is due to the feminine biological fact of giving birth and raising the young, and having to do with Nature rather than Spirit. But not always is the animus dealing with relationships, sometime it represents the spirit of acting and doing in the woman's life. As Emma Jung indicates:[149]

> *"Corresponding to the factual orientation of man and characteristic of the logos principle, the animus can come on the scene in a purely objective, unrelated way, as sage, judge, artist, aviator, mechanic and so on. Not infrequently it appears as a 'stranger'. Perhaps this form in particular is the most characteristic, because, to the purely feminine mind, the spirit stands for what is strange and unknown. The ability to assume different forms seems characteristic of the spirit; like mobility, the power to traverse great distances in a short time, it is expressive of a quality which it shares with light."*

There are animus dreams for women that can give guidance and help in leading her to become more whole in her psychic attitude. But this is not always a smooth or a healthy process, because her ego may resist the dissolution of perceptions dealing with relationships and the known roles that fit her lifestyle. Berry points out what is known among Jungian analysts as the Layard maxim.[150]

> *"The Layard maxim implies that the tensions and conflicts that appear in dreams (and in life) are necessary, even essential. The psyche is deeply complicated, and its tensions are the means by which it moves. The ego alien others who give trouble to the dream ego, sometimes by torturing, are at the same time making possible the individuating movement. The tension is the grist by which the psyche works, the manner in which it enlarges and differentiates itself. This is an individuation without banners, but it is nevertheless, true to the unique personality in all its limitations and particular conflicts. Individuation is the wrestling with the psyche's teleos – even when this teleos runs counter to the ego's natural perspectives and normal behaviors… to work with the Layard maxim means that we may not take our first-level, only-natural feelings too literally."*

What follows is a series of three dreams by a woman over 10 years in which she is led by her animus to deal with perspectives and understanding that will change her psychic attitude toward the spirit with new changes that enter her life, as well as letting go of attachments to her children and her perspectives on reality.

> *4/11/2000 I dreamed that a tall man in a black cape came into a dark room and gave me a puppet. It had a very shiny face and was only painted on half of its face.*

> *2/10/2006 We traveled to 'Appomattox' to visit the man who lived at the corner from us. He was tall and thin and lived a life that was "sustainable" he cooked a soy dish in a large pot and handed me a white plate on which he ladled food and gave me a small spoonful of rice in a yellowish sauce. He said that it was soy based and I said that soy was being planted in the rainforest – to counter his statement. I had to wait to go in the bathroom and when I looked in the mirror at first I thought my eyes were swollen but then I realized that I was Asian.*

> *12/27/2011 I was watching a very tall thin man in a white shirt demonstrating how he can jump off a building and land on his feet. I met him with Miranda (daughter) after the jump. I got to ask him about how he was able to land on his feet. He demonstrated and then fell on Miranda's foot – I woke up.*

In these three dreams the animus or tall male figure introduces her to the figure, which has a painted face, and half is unformed not finished. He is showing the dream ego the duality in the face of life itself, an introduction to her true nature. We must remember that it was Appomattox where North met South to end the civil war. And that East and West, never the twain shall meet. The solution for the dreamer would be to integrate opposites and resolve inner conflict by taking on characteristics of the *other*. In the second dream, the dream ego resists eating foreign food from the guide, a tall man, by pointing out its flaws (where it is from). But then finds out she is Asian anyway and shares the good and bad in herself.

In the third dream, the tall man tries to teach her how to defy the laws of nature and jump. She is interested, but when she approaches his teachings, her attention is taken away from her daughter and she is interrupted in appreciating how to reverse the laws of nature by the emergency caring for her daughter. The third dream has the complement and mythological roots in the cult of Dionysus. Where there is an ecstatic inspiration which seized the dancer (jumper) and she served the god and became filled with spirit.[151] What the spirit has to teach her is a form of dance that is driven by the need to become one with music and like the pied piper of Hamlin, drawn into the depths where the spirit and nature are one – or again having become one.[152] This process of becoming one with the creative spirit is incompatible with nurturing and caring for the other. So there is an inhibition of creativity based on role conflict in the dreamer. Thus, the animus is a guide to wholeness and individuation. To the chagrin of her dream ego, he puts the dreamer to the test. She must lose her relationship dependency with the external world, embrace the duality in her own nature and let her daughter "go" (i.e. not attend to her hurts and accidents) thus opening up the possibility for her own growth into the spirit.

F. Dreams or sleep states can reveal communications with deceased persons

Dreams can be communications from entities beyond the physical plane, i.e. deceased people and other entities from the future not ready to be incarnated. C. G. Jung had broken new psychological ground when he declared in his medical thesis that parapsychological material was not evidence of pathology. In fact his view of spiritualism was that it was evidence of autonomous complexes. Later in his life he dreamed of being a projection of a yogi. In another dream his life was a projection from a UFO. This led him to the conclusion there could be parallel worlds existing simultaneously, one for the deceased and one for the living.[153]

Allan Botkin in his studies with EMDR (Eye Movement Desensitization and Reprocessing) within the Department of Veterans' Affairs discovered with combat trauma veterans a recurring theme... These veterans had unresolved traumatic grief for deceased comrades who died horrible deaths in war. As he employed EMDR, he accidently discovered that by using this method he spontaneously produced in his veteran patients, communication with these deceased war comrades. He developed this method of inducing communication with the dead, through a modified form of EMDR called Induced After Death Communication. He discovered that After Death Communications (ADC) occurred in sleep states:

> *"Sleep state ADCs are very common and occur when a person is asleep, but are experienced as very different from dreams. Like twilight ADCs sleep state ADCs can take on a variety of forms... Twilight ADCs occur just as people are falling asleep or waking up. Any combination of the above ADCs can be involved in this form of ADC."[154]*

Edgar Cayce believed there are 4 reasons why the deceased contact us through dreams:[155]

1. They want something from us, i.e. to help us resolve our feelings about their death by giving us assurance of their wellbeing in other realms of existence.

2. They want to warn us.

3. They may come seeking aid, (as if through prayer)

4. They want to guide us by giving us information.

This last class is amplified by my dream, which predicted the death of my cousin:

> *5/5/1997 I was talking with my dad (who died in 1979). Dad was the narrator and was not visible. He interpreted the image of a young Jack Grove (my cousin) who was seated in the front seat of a car. (Jack was in the car business). Dad was saying, 'he was almost t-boned once'. I got the feeling Jack was dead.*

---

*T-boned is an American expression in the car business meaning being in a wreck and hit by another vehicle at a 90 degree angle usually resulting in severe injury or death.

On December 11, 1997, Jack Grove died of complications of diabetes.

On December 11, 1997 my Radix Age Point and Nodal Age Point were in exact conjunction at 29 degrees of Leo in the 9th house sextile Uranus in the 7th. As Bruno and Louise Huber state, the conjunction of the radix and nodal Age Points represents a crossing on the temporal plane.[156] This conjunction occurred in my 9th house when my fate was sealed by the discovery of my true self's ability to assist (sextile) by an alteration of my awareness (Uranus) in the context of expanding my consciousness and finding my own truth (as represented by the 9th house).[157] Through this dream, I was not only able to bring a message from my deceased father predicting his nephew's death, but pair that with the timing of the crossing of the radix and nodal age points, thus having a very personal message for me... this is what my purpose is – to bring the truth out that dreams and astrology work together in personal development and identifying timing of significant transformative events. This is only accomplished by confidence in a higher power guiding our lives, not the ego from above. As Assagioli calls it, connections with subpersonalities.

> "Psychosynthesis stresses that at their heart subpersonalities have the same archetypal qualities (as in the Jungian sense of universal mythological interpenetration). But when they appear in dreams they bring us messages from the higher unconscious. These messages can include important insights, precognition, telepathy, prophecy and forward relating imagery. Subpersonalities are caught up in the past, either in the more recent past where the dream may be playing out and perhaps re-configuring recent events... The depth work enables the subpersonality to descend into its true inner quality and express it. The height work is to learn to co-operate with archetypes to help clarify issues for subpersonalities." [158]

In psychosynthesis through there is work on the depth and higher work of the Higher Self to achieve true personal integration.

In my life at this time, I was to discover that my true destiny lies in expressing the connections between the living and the dead through dream messages. Their communications reflect my duty as a medium – to share their messages with the living. It is my destiny to discover that my true life's purpose is to share this kind of knowledge with others.

G. Dreams can compensate for one-sided complexes

Complexes are emotionally charged groups of ideas or images in the unconscious. At the 'center' of a complex is an archetype or archetypal image (e.g. Mother who contains a range of contents some of which are opposed to one another such as good-Mother; bad-Mother).[159] These complexes contain emotional valences or constellations of psychic energy that contain dynamic opposites and discharge one of the opposites of the archetype to dramatize a particular problem for the dream ego to solve. Dreams of this type usually reflect a conflict between conscious and unconscious processes. This conflict is resolved in order to orient the consciousness toward wholeness, a process known as individuation. The Self directs this process with or without our conscious participation.[160]

The Self is the archetype of wholeness and the regulating center of the personality. The Self transcends the ego.

Individuation as a goal results in the conscious realization of one's unique psychological reality, including both strengths and limitations. It leads to the experience of the Self as the regulating center of the psyche.[161]

Transformations in consciousness that can come from dreams and the individuation process reveal the 'secret of existence' (which is a) *"continually repeated process of rejuvenation of the psychic system"*. We propose that this process goes on after death.[162]

Dreams come from psychological complexes in the personal unconscious and from the collective unconscious. Dreams can act as compensation in content, balancing the conscious perspective so as to give the dreamer a new perspective on a person or event. They usually take the form of unpleasant images in the dream of the individual challenging him/her to face changes to an old, maladaptive attitude. Taken from the Jungians, it is clear that any psychoanalytic study of dreams leads one to discover that day to day interpreted external events or people are associated with complexes deep within the unconscious. These events actually trigger dreams and complexes. That is the reason that in journaling with a dream diary, it is also necessary to include a daily log of the events of the day so that one can draw correlations from external events that relate to the complex. Dreams often loosen the opposite content in a complex to the conscious standpoint of the waking ego. This is all brought about by an attempt by the psyche to bring about individuation of the ego.

Consider the dream of Amy.[163] *"A man in a black suit is flying away from a witch"* – Amy realized that the suit was like one owned by her father. And despite herself, the witch somehow conjured up her mother. Amy's conscious feelings of hurt, pain, and the determination never to forgive her father (who left her mother) were contradicted by a far different view of her father's behavior in her encoded dream images.

On this unconscious level, Amy saw her father as escaping from a malevolent wife/mother. His escape was a feat of strength and a soaring that suggests Amy's feelings of sympathy and admiration for her father's decision. Although Amy consciously held her father fully responsible for her parents' split up; unconsciously, in her dream, she adopted the diametrically opposite position in which her witch-mother was held more accountable than her father. This type of opposition between conscious and unconscious perceptions, evaluations, and reactions is extremely common.

For days after her father left, Amy picked fights with her female teachers at school. Her unconscious battle with her father – and with her mother – was carried out in a displaced battlefield.

With awareness of the unconscious defenses of projection and displacement of the conflicts that come up in dreams, one can stop attributing to the external world those conflicts which are really intrapsychic and stop self defeating behavior.

Complexes "have a bipolar structure, for example the dominance/submission pattern, where one pole of the relationship is considered dominant, the other submissive. In the impersonal relationship based upon such a pattern, most interactions between the two persons in the relationship will fall into that pattern: one will be submissive, the other dominant. But there are often symptomatic evidences of the reversal of the pattern. For instance, a very successful businessman, who had taken care of everyone around him for decades, retired and found that he had irrational fears of sudden illness in which he would feel helpless and dependent. Discussion revealed that his fear of death was not a major component. What he actually feared was experiencing the opposite (dependent and submissive) identity that he had avoided since an early age by compulsive work and taking care of others."[164]

H. Dreams can lead to Individuation as the emotional attachment to ego identifications wane

Dreams can lead the dreamer on a journey toward individuation, which is a developmental process that in time and through life stages brings psychic functions to their opposite form, manifesting in external events for the purpose of creating wholeness in the psychic system.[165] In this way dreams represent a tendency in the unconscious for changing the conscious attitude. Life transitions from leaving home, having mid life crises, and retirement from the active world are examples of times these dreams seem to show up. When paired with significant planetary and Age Point transits, they reveal an underlying structure of implicit order in our lives.

Feelings of intense conflict about my professional life (a mid life crisis) came about as I was forced to change my role as an Acting Chief Social Worker to Staff Social Worker in 1997 after a management downsizing eliminated the Hospital Social Work Department where I had worked for 11 years. Fiscally conservative government forces generated this. My psychological-developmental task was that I was forced to face an alteration in ego-identity, which changed my role from one of dominance to one of submission.

I had the following dream:

3/20/1997 Reversal of Roles – Was in a room with a clerk. There was a box load of cattle coming to the hospital (where I worked) for surgery with a well-known surgeon. I was taking orders off charts laughing to the clerk (about my role, now like a nurse) saying to the clerk, 'at one time I didn't even answer telephones!'

James Hall states in *Jungian Dream Interpretation*:[166]

"Dreams are not dreamed to be analyzed and understood, but an understanding of dreams tells us where the unconscious is already trying to alter the ego-image in the direction of health and individuation. Health and individuation, however, are not always aligned; what is 'healthy' for the dominant ego image at a particular stage of life may be decidedly unhealthy for the nascent ego image at the next stage of life."

The fact is I did not follow this advice but I resisted where the dream was leading me; now in retrospect, I understand that I should have stayed in my job and 'sucked it up'. This elimination of our department coincided with the crossing of my radix and nodal Age Points, in the 9th house in my house and radix charts. And the message could have been to sustain the loss and become more whole by leaving my leader role and accepting my 'new role'. In January 1997 my house chart, which reflects environmental forces on the native, found a conjunction of these two critical points, and in December 1997 in my radix chart these points were conjunct. This 'crossing point' occurs only once every 36 years and corresponds to the meeting of external events and karmic fate on the temporal plane.[167]

Subsequently, I angrily left the hospital and took a job at another company as Clinical Director of a Psychiatric Partial Hospital Program, which ended up being a disastrous choice. Trying to maintain a position of dominance as Clinical Director by leaving the former job ended in failure. I took a pay cut and I was forced to examine my ethical position in my new job. I was asked to document fraudulent lower functioning scores on the acuity of patients in the medical records so the company would get a higher insurance reimbursement. I could not do this because it was misrepresenting the facts. I went to lawyer and at his advice, left that position after 6 weeks, only to return to my old job exactly in the position of submission I was trying to avoid.

"There are symptomatic evidences of the reversal of the pattern"... from dominance to submission in dreams.[168] And dreams try to prepare one for the developmental change. My fear of facing the change in my ego-image and the demotion of my ego-identity actually propelled me into a job that was "more hot water". My motivation was wrong and I was thrown back on myself to deal with the problem of incognizance to quietly nurture the individuation process. We must all deal with ego losses in the course of life.

If I had known about the Huber Method and these developmental challenges and paired it with my Jungian knowledge of complexes, I could have avoided an expensive and ultimately frustrating return to the self after a complicated digression.

Amplification and the use of active imagination techniques were used by both Jung and Assagioli to work with and find meaning from dreams. Amplification is an imaginal technique that the ego may use to facilitate the experience of true archetypal foundations of psychological complexes such as: guided imagination, drawing, work in clay, gestalt techniques... Active imagination is used for individuation to proceed by the dreamer taking an active stance toward the contents of the objective psyche and making a dialogue with the elements of a dream as they relate to identity and relational structures of the psyche.[169]

Assagioli believed that the middle unconscious structure of the psyche, as depicted in Assagioli's egg diagram[170a], was where dreams come from. In working with dreams one had to distinguish between two types: archetypal and subpersonalities.[170b] The author's shadow dream of Fagin (page 63) represented my subpersonality and would help with integration of personal psychosynthesis.[171]

The following dream is archetypal and has a direct bearing on the individuation process guiding the dreamer through a life transition to retirement:

> *1/19/2014 I had a dream I was going to climb a mountain with some people. We were ascending but I needed clothes. I needed pants and long underwear (security of Saturn). I had a paper bag of money (cash) in which I was going to buy stuff in a store. I left other people I was with to find my gear and got a sense of relief from this. As I wandered through the store alone, I picked up my underwear and jeans. After a discussion with a clerk about something unimportant, I got in line to pay for my stuff. At once I realized that I lost my paper bag of money (security and protection of Saturn). It was gone. I went looking for it. I went back behind the counters and thought one of the clerks took it. I could not find it anywhere. In the end, I had the jeans and the underwear on a table but they belonged to me all along. I did not have to pay for them.*

Interpretation and amplification: I cannot ascend to higher realms with just material means, I must use faith that I will have the resources needed to carry on even when it does not appear to be the case. If I want to climb the mountain (reach a higher spiritual goal), I have to be dressed for it (preparation for the journey); but I should not be distracted if the means is immediately unavailable to outfit myself. I should discover a new way of knowledge to perceive the problem of reaching the heights without the protection of money. On January 31, 2014 I retired from my employment and in that transition to reach for material security in order to find wholeness, I must let go of attachments represented by money. As most of us know, when one retires, one has less material resources. Aspects that are relevant were the Neptune transits in the 3rd house (my communications, immediate environment) opposed natal Saturn in the 9th house (security, philosophy, publishing, etc) aspect now triggers my awareness of the illusionary protection (Neptune oppose Saturn) that the material plane provides. This transit and the dream together tell the solution: don't worry about the money, move forward with your spiritual goals.

Consider the journey (mountain climbing) preparing for the feat by having the right tools (underclothing) and the means needed to prepare (i.e. money was not needed); it was the *will* to accomplish the goal of retirement. The previous dream is archetypal because it has universal and mythological elements found in many stories worldwide: preparation for a journey, meager means to accomplish it based on assumptions of the material world, and use of the will and only the will that will get one through to accomplish the goal. This theme is similar to many hero myths.

As applied to the psychosynthesis model, this dream is a message from the transpersonal or spiritual self[172] translated to the middle unconscious in imagery of a journey that represents my retirement and goals beyond it. To awaken our knowledge from dreams and receive guidance from the transpersonal self is within the reach of all of us and is the main purpose of this work. Through dream interpretation paired with significant transitions in our lives (as exemplified by planetary transits), each one of us has access to the insights and inspirations of the transpersonal self through archetypal dreams. Through dreams, one has to awaken the will to apply our dream material to significant events in our lives and imbue our lives with direction for higher spiritual development.

"The correct use of the will and imagination (dreams) awakens the higher centers in the human system that bring responsibilities of a deeper nature."[173]

Our responsibility is to listen to the archetypal dreams and use our will to study and receive guidance from the transpersonal self.

I. Traumatic Dreams

Dreams are sometimes traumatic, and reflect real traumas that have occurred and are repressed or suppressed in conscious life. These are repetitive and take the form of nightmares, which reflect actual events of the trauma. Dreams of actual fire fights in war are a common focus in trauma in the treatment of post traumatic stress disorder among former combatants. In these firefights there were many casualties of comrades; these traumatic memories can plague the survivors with distorted feelings of self blame which can trigger depression. The unresolved feelings of guilt can create ego dystonic states that can persist in recurrent depressions.[174]

As illustrated earlier with the work of Dr. Allan Botkin, he used EMDR in treating the post traumatic stress disorder. And later Dr. Botkin through the use of modified EMDR techniques with the same patients, worked on resolving traumatic grief by having the deceased comrades 'visit' his patients in images and communications to actually resolve their distressing traumatic memories and survival guilt. Dr Botkin helped patients to stop these disturbing and anxiety provoking traumatic nightmares. Botkin had used a technical EMDR maneuver after he resolved the trauma, to elicit visitations from the dead Vietnam veterans who as subpersonalities were needing to break through to resolve survival guilt in their buddies.

Psychosynthesis employs visualizations *"as induction techniques in which the therapist picks up the dream image last dreamt. The patient is asked to allow, follow and engage in whatever images and senses emerge from their unconscious. Whatever happens in the dream is encouraged to unfold freely through the use of a few well-chosen supportive interventions. Than after a while the dreamer is gently led back to consciousness in the room, where the telling of the dream or imagery, its interpretation and other dream work can begin."* [175]

A researched technique used by the Department of Veterans' Affairs with good results in resolving traumatic dreaming without the use of medication employs telling the patient before the induction described above to let the images flow but at the end, when tragedy occurred, change the ending to something positive. The treatment is Imagery Rehearsal Therapy (IRT). In IRT, the person who is having nightmares, while awake, changes how the nightmare ends so that it no longer upsets them. Then the person replays over and over in their minds the new dream with the non-scary ending. Research shows that this type of treatment can reduce how often nightmares occur.[176] Neutralizing traumatic dreams is then completed by re-writing the dream with the different, and positive ending. This can effect traumatic, repeating dreams by neutralizing the valence of the disturbing trauma complex induced content.

Conclusion

The dreams presented here are the author's own and those of close personal contacts. The synchronistic pairing of recorded dreams and interpretations throughout a life with Age Point progressions, transits of planets and crossing points in natal/nodal charts provides an orientation through the maze of developmental challenges that the individual faces. This process leads to wholeness and psychological balance – individuation as Jung calls it. The shadow, the anima, the animus, the unconscious parts of ourselves can be disorienting as they possess us and command our attention by their projections onto others. There is so little attention given to the working out of these inner influences and I have been taken to task to provide that work.

The call of the individual Self to wholeness is made comprehensible from the youth leaving home, finding a partner – to balancing the opposite tendencies of the psychological functions after midlife. It is the purpose of this work to provide some direction for others about this process by pairing the study of dreams with significant astrological events. In that way the transformation toward wholeness, that alchemical process of individuation, becomes comprehensible and acceptable. No longer is the individual alone in the enchanted forest with sinuous paths and a direction unknown. Instead, we can provide a path toward wholeness that is understandable and which brings meaning and significance to the individual lives on mythological journeys.

Appendix 1 – Triple Charts for John D. Grove

Following are radix, nodal and house charts for the author.

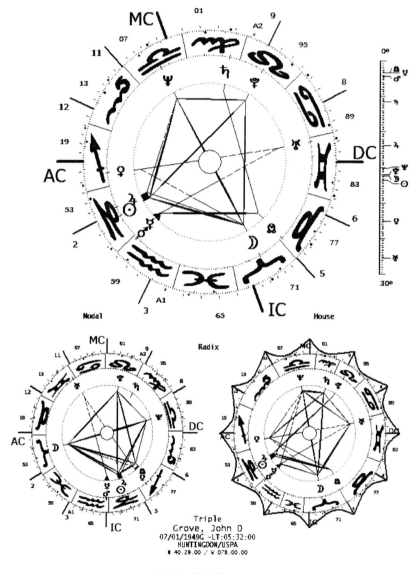

John D. Grove
07.01.1949, 05:32, Huntingdon, PA, USA

Appendix 2 Psychological Astrology:
Signs, Planets and Houses

How to discern symbolic meanings of Planets, Signs and Houses for your own lives.

These notes are based on teaching material used by Dr Maureen Demot, my former teacher in Jungian Astrological Psychology. Maureen Demot died in a car crash in February 2001.

ARIES

Psychological Need/ Motivation:	Survival, Freedom, Independence, Immediate gratification
Archetypes:	Warrior, Pioneer, Noble Savage, Adventurer, Explorer
Developmental Stage:	Birth to 18 months. Need for basic trust. Primary Narcissism. Undifferentiated Self. Sense of omnipotence.
Behavioural Traits:	Assertive, egocentric, primitive, innocent, independent, direct, energetic, decisive, initiating, impulsive, fearless, impatient
Pathology:	Anti-social personality disorder. Impulse disorder. Sociopathic personality. The essential feature is a history of hostile and aggressive behaviour in which the rights of others are violated.

MARS

Psychological Function:	Survival instinct, assertion, aggression, initiative, Id, Libido, drive, Competitive instinct.
Psychological Process:	To assert. to initiate, to vitalize, to act, to do, to endeavour.
Psychological States:	Aliveness, joi de vivre, vitality, energy, impetuousness, decisiveness, omnipotence, impulsiveness, recklessness, impatience, selfishness, aggression, irritability, anger.
Environmental Events:	New enterprises or projects, adventures, fights, competitions, accidents, headaches, high blood pressure, mechanical ability, engineering skill, "do it yourself" type work.

FIRST HOUSE

Persona. Surface personality, how we initiate and assert, how others see us initially (first impression), instinctual expression, spontaneous action, initial impulse, first step forward, body language, what we need and What we do to survive as a separate entity. Focus on adventure, freedom, autonomy.

TAURUS

Psychological Need/ Motivation:	Safety, Security, Stability, Sensual Gratification, Pleasure,
Archetypes:	Earth Mother, Fertility Goddess, Settler, Sensualist, Glutton
Developmental Stage:	18 months to 4 years, Focus on self and object constancy
Behavioural Traits:	Sensuous, attractive, materialistic, concrete, calm, stable, placid, steadfast, plodding, patient, enduring, conservative, possessive, retentive, attached, resistive to change, stubborn
Pathology:	Borderline personality. Key feature: insecurity

VENUS

Psychological Function:	Self and Object Constancy, Personal Security, Stability
Psychological Process:	To acquire (things), to have, to secure, to accumulate, to soothe, to comfort, to pleasure oneself; to gratify
Psychological States:	Safety security, comfort, pleasure, serenity, equanimity, self-indulgence, laziness, lethargy, resistence, gluttony, greed
Environmental Events:	Accumulation of goods and money; experiences that provide for security, pleasure and comfort

SECOND HOUSE

Approach to money, physical resources, possessions; that which gives pleasure, comfort and security. One's attitude toward the physical body and bodily needs (sensual gratification). Focus on attachment and ownership. Issues around safety and stability. The way one acquires physical security and possessions, and what one acquires.

GEMINI

Psychological Need/ Motivation:	Information, Data, Factual Knowledge, Learning, Mental Stimulation, Communication, Language
Archetypes:	Messenger, Reporter, Student, Amateur, Puer Aeternus
Developmental Stage:	4 to 7 years. Learning to read & write. Stage of curiosity and development. Explosion of learning.
Behavioural Traits:	Curious, communicative, bright, precocious, restless, witty, hyperactive, knowledgeable (about factual matters), versatile, adroit, superficial, chatty, glib, fickle, light, flighty, scattered
Pathology:	(ADHD) Learning Disorder.

MERCURY

Psychological Function:	Cognition, Thinking, Intellect, Reason, Mentation, Wit
Psychological Process:	To learn, to enquire, to study, to define, to label & classify, to communicate, to report, to inform (get the message out)
Psychological States:	Curiosity, interest, attentive, verbosity, restlessness, nervousness, restlessness, hyperactive, scatteredness
Environmental Events:	Any learning situation. Involvement in communications media - writing, reporting, journalism, research. Classifying and filing of information. Being an amateur, dilettante, or jack-of-all-trades (master of none).

THIRD HOUSE

Focus on acquiring and communicating information. Day to day thinking. Rote leaning and early school experiences. Data gathering, writing, and reporting. Getting the message out. Short distance travel. Sibling relationships. Neighbours.

CANCER

Psychological Need/ Motivation:	Nurturing, Care, Tenderness, Unconditional Love, Belonging, Sympathetic Understanding, Closeness, Emotional Support
Archetypes:	Mother, Caretaker, Dependent Children, Wombs, Containers.
Developmental Stage:	8 to 12 years. Period of introspection. Consolidation of super-ego (self-inhibition). Capacity to contain and reflect on feelings
Behavioural Traits:	Nurturing, caring, protective, tender, soft, sensitive, gentle, receptive, mirroring, reactive, impressionable, indirect, shy, timid, introverted, sentimental, vulnerable, dependent
Pathology:	Histrionic Personality Disorder Essential feature: Dependency. In extreme: Avoidant Personality Disorder

MOON

Psychological Function:	Receptive Function, Listening Response, Nurturing Faculty, Memory, Personal Unconscious
Psychological Process:	To nurture and protect, to listen and understand, to reflect, to remember, to sympathize, to accept and love unconditionally
Psychological States:	Loving feelings, belonging, closeness, warmth and tenderness. Vulnerability to rejection, dependency, self-protectiveness
Environmental Events:	Relations with mother/women. Restaurant work, caretaking work, activity that involves nurturing & protecting (feeding, housing, or providing emotional support)

FOURTH HOUSE

Mother, personal past, nesting experience, family, roots, foundations, early childhood experiences of nurturing., home, domestic conditions (past and present). Sense of belonging. Real estate and other activities having to do with the land, or homeland (patriotism).

LEO

Psychological Need/ Motivation:	Validation of Identity, Self-esteem, Approval, Attention, Creative, Self-expression, Enjoyment of Self and Others
Archetypes:	Heroes & Heroines, Star Performer, Romantic, Peacock, Playmate
Developmental Stage:	12 to 18 years (adolescence). Consolidation of identity, Separation from family matrix (counterdependent). Emphasis on peer relations
Behavioural Traits:	Proud, confident, playful, affable, magnanimous, creative, expressive, dramatic, positive, overbearing, showy, boastful, naive (uncritical), egocentric, defensive, prideful
Pathology:	Narcissistic Personality. "Divinity complex" Over-compensation for unconscious fear that one has no value, importance, or worth.

SUN

Psychological Function: Ego, Identity, Self-Concept, Creativity, Intention, Wilt, Volition

Psychological Process: To create, to express, to intend, to choose, to play, to validate (others), to impress (seek approval), to defend (self), to romance

Psychological States: Pride and Self-esteem (vs Shame), Confidence (vs Self-doubt), Playfulness, Willfulness, vitality, creativity, Arrogance, Conceit.

Environmental Events: Father/Men, Play and Playmates, Fun and Games, Romance & Courtship, Good Times, Sports, Hedonism, Extravagance

FIFTH HOUSE

Creative self-expression or performance via theatre, teaching, or the arts. Our subjective perception of "audience," e.g. fans, spectators, supporters, detractors. Experiences of validation of invalidation, especially through romance and courtship. One's romantic interest. All forms of play and recreation - parties, vacation, fun & games, entertainment, sports, gambling, and speculation. Playmates, bosom buddies. The results of creativity, including one's children.

VIRGO

Psychological Need/ Motivation:	Efficient functioning, competency, to be of service, improvement
Archetypes:	Efficiency Expert, Troubleshooter, Fix It Man, Apprentice/Novice, Doubting Thomas, Analyst, Critic, Worry Wart, Spinster
Developmental Stage:	19 to 26 years. Novice stage of adulthood. Period of apprenticeship. Developing a skill or trade and entering the work force. Service.
Behavioural Traits:	Efficient, competent, pragmatic, conscientious, helpful, technical, precise, systematic, orderly, humble, modest, skeptical, restrained, analytical, discriminating, critical, picky, fastidious, meticulous.
Pathology:	Obsessive/Compulsive Personality Disorder. Extreme preoccupation with trivial details, rules, order, schedules etc.

MERCURY

Psychological Function:	Cognition, Intellect. Discrimination. Analysis. Problem Solving
Psychological Process:	To analyze and criticize, to reduce (to parts), to correct or fix, to solve, to improve, to serve, to discriminate.
Psychological States:	Feeling useful/productive. State of efficiency/ competence_ Negative, critical mind-set. Worrying, pondering, figuring, analyzing, obsessing.
Environmental Events:	Problems that need solving. Things that need fixing. Mistakes that correcting. Any kind of work or service, especially crafts, trades, merchandising, and the health field, e.g., diet and nutrition.

SIXTH HOUSE

Mundane, day to day responsibilities - chores, tasks, attending to details. Health and hygiene. Repair and maintenance department. Work and relations with co-workers/employees. Being of service to the community. Focus on tasks and getting the job done. Employment history.

LIBRA

Psychological Need/ Motivation:	Harmony, Beauty, Intimacy, Companionship, Relatedness, Fairness
Archetypes:	Love Goddess, 'Beloved, Peacemaker, Mediator, Diplomat, Public Relations Person, Networker, Social Butterfly, Artist
Developmental Stage:	26 to 35 years. Emergence into full adult status as "social equal." Increased ethical sense. Emphasis on partnership. Networking phase.
Behavioural Traits:	Engaging, charming, nice, sociable, polite, tactful, graceful, aesthetic, tactful, appealing, fair, just, impartial, considerate, cooperative, thoughtful, placating, superficial, compliant, indecisive, equivocating
Pathology:	Dependent Personality Disorder. Over-compliant, appeasing, conciliatory behaviour.

VENUS

Psychological Function:	Aesthetic Function ("taste"), Artistic Sense, Social Ability
Psychological Process:	To beautify, to balance, to harmonize; to cooperate, to consider; to mediate, to negotiate;. to attract and engage; to socialize.
Psychological States:	Love and affection; intimacy, harmony, cooperation; grace and charm; aesthetic appreciation, love and beauty; serenity, equanimity; overdependencey on others for love and connection.
Environmental Events:	All relationships of partnership or cooperation with "equal others." Contracts, agreements (or conflicts, lawsuits); social connections and networking; pursuit of beauty, artistic endeavours

SEVENTH HOUSE

Partner or open enemy. The "not-self," i.e. qualities we project, attract, and evoke in other people. Contracts and agreements. Marriage/divorce. Public relations and networking in general. Ability to socialize and conform to social amenities. Social contract. Art, Beauty, aesthetics.

SCORPIO

Psychological Need/ Transformation, Healing, Reform, Catharsis,
Motivation: Elimination, Sexuality, Power through union with
the unknown (shadow). Integrity.

Archetypes: Wounded Healer, Shaman, Shadow Figures,
Monsters & Villains, Underworld Figures,
Erotic Types, Tyrants, The Stranger.

Developmental Stage: 35 to 45 years. Mid-life crisis. Facing one's mortality
and unlived self. Period of self-renewal. Becoming
authentic. Owning our power.

Behavioural Traits: Erotic, provocative, penetrating, suspicious,
guarded, intense, deep, dark, passionate, controlling,
dangerous, covert, tactical, manipulative, vindictive,
extreme, daemonic, exposing, regenerative.

Pathology: Paranoid Personality. In milder form; control issues.

PLUTO

Psychological Function: Sexuality, Eros, Power, Healing Function, Shadow,
Wound.

Psychological Process: To penetrate, to assimilate, to integrate; to
transform, to heal, to regenerate; to purify, to
cleanse, to eliminate; to fear, to distrust; to control,
to coerce, to dominate; to scheme, to sabotage, to
destroy.

Psychological States: Crisis, Fear, Paranoia, Trauma, Pain and Suffering,
Sexual Passion, Possessed by the dark side. Intensity,
Focus, Power, Integrity.

Environmental Events: Dealing with crisis, facing one's fears. Power
struggles, control issues. Tyranny, crime, subversion,
evil. Descent to the underworld and confronting the
shadow. Any kind of healing or reforming work.

EIGHTH HOUSE

Sexuality. Crisis intervention work (paramedics, fireman, police).
Healing relationships (doctors, therapists). Shared financial relationships
(investments, taxes, debts). Personal taboos, shadows, and wounds. Interest
in matters pertaining to danger, death, the occult, or simply the unknown.

SAGITTARIUS

Psychological Need/ Motivation:	Truth, Meaning, Purpose, Justice, Virtue, Morality, Expansion.
Archetypes:	Teacher, Guru, Prophet, Demagogue, Moralist, Pollyanna.
Developmental Stage:	45 to 56 years. Age wisdom and influence, insightfulness and philosophic concern. True integrity. Becoming a grandparent.
Behavioural Traits:	Jovial, enthusiastic, optimistic, philosophical, opinionated, truthful, frank, moralistic, righteous, persuasive, expansive, idealistic, inspired, travel-loving, benevolent, philanthropic, excessive, grandiose, manic.
Pathology:	Manic Syndrome. Inflation.

JUPITER

Psychological Function:	Judgment, Higher Mind, Morality, Conscience, Faith, Hope.
Psychological Process:	To judge, to theorize, to interpret (explain); to teach, to preach, to affirm as right or true; to predict; to trust, to hope, to have faith; to expand or broaden; to overextend and exaggerate.
Psychological States:	Hope, optimism, enthusiasm, great expectations (fairy godmother complex), trust in the Universe; wisdom, foresight; grandiosity, dogmatism, extravagance, blind optimism, manic.
Environmental Events:	Good luck; philanthropic activities; act of influencing or persuading others of some truth; religious or philosophical practices; encounters with teachers; consequences of excess or extravagance.

NINTH HOUSE

Experiences in higher education, philosophy, or religion. Approach to matter of faith, ideology, ethics, and values. Encounters with teachers, Truth seeking. Scholarship. Concerns about justice and legality. Dissemination of knowledge though teaching, publishing, promotion, or advertising. Travel, sacred journeys, and other mind expanding experiences.

CAPRICORN

Psychological Need/ Motivation:	Perfection, Success, Structure, Order, Control, Authority.
Archetypes:	Senex, Father Figure, Authority Figure, Control Freak, Scrooge
Developmental Stage:	56 to 68 years. Period of highest career achievement. Zenith of one's life. Antithesis of success is despair and regret. Final reckoning.
Behavioural Traits:	Serious, reserved, formal, ambitious, persevering, perfectionistic, exacting, focused, fastidious, orderly, organized, disciplined, planful. practical, realistic, traditional, conservative, prudent, callous, grim.
Pathology:	Dysthymia (depression). Workaholism, pessimism, obsessive-compulsive neurosis.

SATURN

Psychological Function:	Sense of Duty, Ambition, Self-Discipline, Self-Control, Limits
Psychological Process:	To achieve, to succeed, to persevere, to structure, to order, to manage, to plan, to control, to perfect, to master, to fear, to inhibit, to restrict, to contract, to deprive, to crave, to overcompensate.
Psychological States:	Success, mission accomplished, patient, in control, determined, dutiful, obligated, pressured, driven, anxious, inferior, inadequate, deficient, defective, negative, pessimistic, gloomy, lonely, despair.
Environmental Events:	Experiences of limitation, delay, deficiency, Obstacles, blocks, and restrictions. Responsibilities, duties, Success through perseverance, or failure through procrastination and fear.

TENTH HOUSE

Career, vocation, dominant goal. Potential for success. Ultimate impact one has upon society. Reputation, public image, honours, status, distinctions. Dominant other, attitude toward authority and limits. Father, bosses, superiors. Capacity for and the way one handles authority.

AQUARIUS

Psychological Need/ Motivation:	Awakening, Revelation, Perspective, Liberation, Change, Progress
Archetypes:	Trickster, Objective Witness, Prometheus, Revolutionary, Radical, Humanitarian, Utopian Visionary, Mad Scientist, Eccentric, Oddball.
Developmental Stage:	68 to 80 years. Seeing one's life as a whole. Radical objectivity. Eccentricity of old age. Outspokenness. Detachment from ego.
Behavioural Traits:	Detached, objective, cool, whimsical, broad-minded, non-judgmental, impersonal, eccentric, original, innovative, progressive, humanitarian, altruistic, rebellious, outspoken, enlightening, shocking, erratic.
Pathology:	Schizoid Personality Disorder. "Social misfit," Schizoid detachment. Behaviour is unpredictable.

URANUS

Psychological Function:	Observing Ego, Objective, Witness, Universal Mind, Altruism, Wholistic Thinking, Radical insight, Capacity for Change.
Psychological Process:	To awaken, to enlighten, to liberate, to change, to progress, to advance, to rebel, to agitate, to disrupt.
Psychological States:	Altruistic love (agape), sudden flash of insight, realization, detached overview, choiceless awareness, liberation, dissent, agitation, upset, startled, shock, unstable, schizoid detachment.
Environmental Events:	Sudden change in a system, instability, the unexpected. Something bizarre, strange, extraordinary. Anything involving advanced technology. A revolution Of breakthrough or breakdown,

ELEVENTH HOUSE

Ideals and aspirations for humanity as a whole. Friends of like mind bound together for a common cause. Movements, humanitarian concerns, group associations. Activities on the cutting edge of change with colleagues and associates. Progressive ideas, visions for the future, altruistic acts.

PISCES

Psychological Need/ Motivation:	Transcendence, Unity, Infinite Love & Beauty, Oneness with nature,
Archetypes:	Mystic, Saviour, Rescuer, Martyr, Victim, Poet, Dreamer, Fraud.
Developmental Stage:	80 to end of life. Collapsing of boundaries in time and space. Diffuse awareness. Confusion, deterioration, loss, senility, infirmity, decay.
Behavioural Traits:	Passive, submissive, delicate, dreamy, yielding, compassionate, empathetic, forgiving, sensitive, global, vague, confused, vacillating, imaginative, inspiring, idealistic, escapist, spiritual, intuitive, psychic.
Pathology:	Schizophrenia (Psychosis). Based on desire to escape reality. Symptoms: hallucinations, illogical thinking, multiple delusions.

NEPTUNE

Psychological Function:	Collective Unconscious, Imagination, Empathy, Dreams, Intuition.
Psychological Process:	To transcend, to surrender, to sacrifice; to empathize, to rescue; to imagine, to envision, to dream, to inspire; to escape, to deny; to vacillate, to sabotage, to confuse, to mystify, to deceive.
Psychological States:	Selfless love, unitive awareness, empathy, compassion, forgiveness, inspiration, GUILT, passivity, confusion, uncertainty, grief, sickness, victimization, helplessness, delusion.
Environmental Events:	Spiritual pursuits, aspire to an ideal; rescuing or helping victims; victim of fraud or deceit; losses, endings, working with grief; use of the imagination, imaginistic art forms (film, painting).

TWELFTH HOUSE

The collective unconscious, mysticism. Service of a selfless or spiritual nature. Charity work. Places of solitude & escape - retreats, the wilderness. Places of incarceration - hospitals, shelters, prisons. Sacrifice, victimization, self-undoing. Transcendent creativity - poetry, film, music, dance. Working with the unconscious, dream analysis, intuition training, psi phenomena.

Notes

1.   Wikipedia, Zeitgeist

2.   Freud, Anna. *Ego Psychology*. 1972

3.   Assagioli, Roberto, MD, T*ranspersonal Development*. Smiling Wisdom. Forres, Scotland. 2007 p. 118

4.   Myss, Caroline. *Defy Gravity*. Hay House Inc. 2009.

5.   Jung, C. G. *The Undiscovered Self*, Bolingen Series XX, 1958, Princeton, N. J. p. 135.

6.   Jung, C. G. *Memories, Dreams and Reflections*, Vantage books, New York, 1961 , p.331

7.   Thompson, William Irwin, *New Story*, "It Has Already Begun- The Planetary Age is an Unacknowledged Daily Reality". 1986

8.   Ibid.

9.   Hawkins, David. *Transcending the Levels of Consciousness.*, Veritus Publishing. W. Sedona , Arizona. 2009.p. 167

10.   Hopewell, Joyce and Llewellyn, Richard, *The Cosmic Egg Timer*, HopeWell, Knutsford,England. 2004.

11a   Jung, C.G. *The Interpretation and Nature of the Psyche*, Synchronicity and Acausal Connecting Principle, Bolengen Series LI, Pantheon Books, NY 1955 p146

11b   Bair, Deirdre, *Jung, A Biography*, Back Bay Books, New York and Boston, 2004, pps. 550-551

12.   Le Grice, Keiron, *The Archetypal Cosmos*. Floris Books, Great Briton, 2010 p. 212-213

13.   Huber, Hopewell, Joyce and Llewellyn, Richard, *The Cosmic Egg Timer*, HopeWell, Knutsford, England. 2004, pps127-128

14.   Huber, Bruno and Louise, *The Astrological Houses*, Samuel Weiser, Inc. York Beach, Maine, 1998 p. 23

15.   Hopewell, Joyce and Llewellyn, Richard; *The Cosmic Egg Timer*, HopeWell, Knutsford, England. P. 16.

16.   Jung, C. G. *The Undiscovered Self*, Vols 10 and 18 Bollingen Series, Princeton University Press, Princeton, NJ, 1958 pps. 121, 127

17.   Jung, C. G. *Psychological Types*, Bollingen Foundation, Princeton University Press Princeton, N. J., 1923.

18.   Thompson, William. Op. Cit.

19.   Ibid.

20. Jung, C. G. *Memories, Dreams and Reflections*, Vantage Books, New York, 1961 ,p. 196

21. Tarnas, Richard. *Cosmos and Psyche*. Penguin Books, London, England. 2007. P. 40

22. Op. Cit. Hopewell and Llwellyn.

23. Jung, C. G. *The World Within*, In His Own Words. DVD. 2008

24. Zap, Jonathon. *Crossing the Event Horizon*. 2012. p. 115

25. Ibid.

26. Ibid. p. 116

27. Jung, C. G. *Aion*. Bollingen Foundation. New York, New York. 1959. P. 168

28. McLuhan, Marshall. *The Medium is the Message*, Signet Books, New York. 1964

29. Hillman, James, *Healing Fiction*, Spring Publications. Putnam, Conn. 1994 pps100-102

30. Ibid. p. 103

31. Op. Cit. Jung *Aion*. P. 165

32. Thompson, William Irwin, *Emergence of Ego and Empire on to Human Individuation*. Today's Preposterous. August 6,2010, Blog

33. Op. Cit. Hopewell and Llwellyn. *The Cosmic Egg Timer*

34. Ibid. p. 144-145

35. Ibid. p. 150-151

36. Ibid.

37. Ibid. p. 145

38a Huber, Bruno & Louise, *The Astrological Houses*, Samuel Weiser 1998, pps 81-87

38b Jacobi, Jolande. *The Psychology of C. G. Jung*, Yale University Press. New Haven. London, p. 135 1973

39. Hall, James A. *The Jungian Experience*, Inner City Books, Toronto, Canada, 1986. P 105

40. Huber, Bruno and Louise, *Moon Node Astrology*. HopeWell, Knutsford, England. 2005

41. Huber, Bruno and Louise and Michael, *Aspect Pattern Astrology*. HopeWell, Knutsford, England. 2005

42. Op. Cit. Hopewell and Llewellyn. *The Cosmic Egg Timer*, p. 14

43. Op. Cit. Zap. P. 8

44. Op. Cit. Hubers. *Aspect Pattern Astrology*

45. McTaggart, Lynne, *The Field*, Harper, New York, 2008

46. Ibid.

47. Boring, E. G. (1950) *History of Experimental Psychology*, (pp. 160-178) New York, Appleton Century Crofts.

48. Diamond, S. (1980) in Wundt before Leipzig in R. W. Rieber (Ed.) *William Wundt in the Making of a Scientific Psychology.* (pp. 3-36, 43-46, 58-63) New York: Plenam Press

49. *Internet Encyclopedia of Philosophy.* Leibinz Metaphysics. Introduction.

50. Charet, F. X., *Spiritualism and the Foundations of C. G. Jung's Psychology*, State University of New York, Albany. 1993. (P. 114)

51. Ibid. p. 100.

52. Wenzel,Amy;Brown, Gregory; Karlin,Bradley. US Department of Veterans Affairs. *Cognitive Behavioral Therapy for Depression in Veterans and Military Service Members*, Washington, D.C. 2011.

53. Op.Cit. Assagnioli, Roberto, *Transpersonal Development.* P.34

54. Wikipedia, John Calvin and Predestination.

55. Weber, Max. *Protestantism and the Rise of Capitalism.* 1930. Routledge, Taylor and Francis Group. New York, New York.

56. Chevalier, Christopher. *Manifest Destiny*, Hubris, Civil Liberties and oh, yes Captain Prichard. 3/19/2010. Blog.

57. Hawkins, David R. *The Eye of the I.* Veritas Publishing, W. Sedona, Arizona. 2001. P. 10.

58. Hawkins, David R. *Transcending the Levels of Consciousness.* Veritas Publishing. W. Sedona, Arizona, 2006. P.100

59. Op. Cit. Tarnas, Richard. *Cosmos and Psyche.* P. 35.

60. Benson, H. *Beyond the Relaxation Response.* Signet Books, New York, New York. P. 17.

61. Whitmont, E.C. and Perear, B. S. *Dreams a Portal to the Source.* Routledge, London. 1989. P. 17.

62. Nowlin, J. B. *The Association of Nocturnal Angina Pectoris with Dreaming.* Annals of Internal Medicine. Pp. 1040-1044. December 1965

63. Jung, C. G. The Significance of Dreams, *The Undiscovered Self in The Collective Works of C.G. Jung.* Bollengin Series XX. 1990.p. 65.

64. Jacobi, Jolande. *The Psychology of C.G. Jung.* Diagram 6. Book Crafters, Inc. Chelsea, Michigan, 1973. P. 130.

65.   Hall, James A. *Jungian Dream Interpretation.* Inner City Books. Toronto, Canada. 1983. P. 9.

66.   Ibid. p. 10

67.   Ibid. p. 12.

68.   Jung, C.G. *Aion*. Bollengin Foundation. Princeton, N. J. 1959. P. 179

69.   Ibid.

70.   Hall, James A. *Jungian Dream Interpretation.* Inner City Books, Toronto, Canada. 1983.p. 120.

71.   Demot, Maureen, *Psychological Astrology: Signs, Planets and Houses*; 2000. Appendix 2.

72.   Martin, Joel and Romanowski, Patricia; *WE Don't Die*, George Anderson's Conversations with the Other Side, Berkley Books, New York, 1989

73.   Swartz, Gary E. *The Afterlife Experiments* Atria Books, New York. 2002. P. 267-268.

74.   Charet, F. X. *Spiritualism and the Foundations of Jung's Psychology.* State University of New York Press, Albany. USA. 1993. P. 270.

75.   Jung, C. G. *Memories Dreams and Reflections* Vantage Books. New York, New York. 1965.p.296.

76.   Jung letters 2, 1951-1961. P. 561

77.   Op. Cit. Swartz. P 267

78.   Botkin, Allan. *Induced After Death Communication* Hampton Roads. Publishing Company Inc. Charlottesville, VA. USA.2005. P. xix

79.   Wikipedia, Reincarnation Research. Internet. 2013.

80.   Huber, Bruno and Louise. *Moon Node Astrology: The Inner Compass of Evolution.* Hopewell, Knutsford, England. 1995. P.140

81.   Jung, C. G. *Synchronicity: An Acausal Connecting Principle.* Bollingen Foundation . Princeton, N.J. 1955

82.   Sadu, Mouni, *Meditation.* Wilshire Book Company. Hollywood California, 1967. P. 31

83.   Tarnas, Richard *Cosmos and Psyche* Penguin Books, London. 2006. P. 481

84.   Op. Cit. *The Afterlife Experiments.* P. 266

85.   http://amaranthpublishing.com/kepler.htm

86. Jung, C.G. *The Red Book*. Ed. Shumdasani, Sonu; Appendix B. Commentaries. W.W. Norton and Company. New York. London. 2009.

87. Rudhyar, Dane. *Transpersonal Astrology*. The Seed Center. Palo Alto, California. 1975. P. 21

88. Jung, C. G. *The Red Book*. Ed. Shumdasani, Sonu; Appendix B. Commentaries. W.W. Norton and Company. New York. London. 2009. Pps. 366-367

89. Op. Cit. *Synchronicity and Acasual Connecting Principle*

90. Wikepedia. Bruno Huber. The Huber School. Internet. 2013

91. Rudhyar, Dane, *An Astrological Study of Psychological Complexes*, Shambhala, Berkeley. 1976

92. Le Grice, Keiron, *The Archetypal Cosmos*, Floris Books, 2010, p. 246.

93. Hopewell, Joyce and Llewellyn, Richard, *The Cosmic Egg Timer*, HopeWell, Knutsford, England, 2004. Pp. 127-128

94. Ibid.

95. Jung, C. G. *Aion*, Bollingen Series XX, Princeton University Press, Princeton, NJ. 1978, p. 8

96. Op. Cit. *Moon Node Astrology*: An Inner Compass of Evolution

97. Hopewell, Joyce *The Living Birth Chart*. HopeWell, Knutford England.2008 p.102

98. Hall, James A. *Jungian Dream Interpretation*. Inner City Books, Toronto, Canada, 1983, p. 128

99. Op. Cit. pp 30-31

100. Vedfelt, Ole. *The Dimensions of Dreams: the Nature, Function and Interpretation of Dreams* Fromm International Publishing Company. Portland, Oregon. 2001.

101. Op. Cit. Progoff. *Intensive Journal Workbook*.Daily Log section.

102. Progoff Intensive Journal Program, Dialogue House Associates, Inc. 80 East 11th street- suite 305, New York, N Y

103. Op. Cit. Progoff. *At a Journal Workshop*.

104. Manas, Volume XL, No. 39 September 10,1987.

105. Op. Cit. Hopewell and Llewellyn. *The Cosmic Egg Timer*

106. Erickson, Erik. *Childhood and Society. Identity vs. Role Confusion*. Norton Publishers. NY. NY. 1993

107. Op. Cit. Hall. *Jungian Dream Interpretation* p 49

108. Op. Cit. Demot. *Psychological Astrology: Sign, Planets and Houses.* Neptune and Moon. Appendix I

109. Doors, Lyrics by Jim Morrison. Yes, The River Knows. Waiting for the Sun. Elektra Records. 1968

110. Op. Cit. Hall.

111. 90 Kingsley, Charles. *The Water Babies, A Fairy Tale for a Land Baby.* In Macmillan's Magazine. London. 1863

112. Op. Cit. Hall. *Jungian Dream Interpretation* P. 120.

113. Ibid. p. 31

114. Op. Cit. Huber. *Moon Node Astrology.* P. 145

115. Jung, C. G. In a letter to a patient.

116. Adler, G. ed., Letters. C.G. Jung. Princeton University Press. Princeton, N. J. 1973 p. 254

117. Johnson, Robert A. *Inner Work.* Harper and Row publishers, San Francisco. 1986

118. Op. Cit. *Moon Node Astrology.* P. 147

119. Hillman, James. *Healing Fiction.* Spring Publications. Putnam, Conn. USA. 1994 p. 54

120. Ibid. P. 55

121. Ibid.

122. Ulanov, Ann Belford, *The Feminine in Jungian Psychology and in Christian Theology.* Northewestern University Press, Evanston, Ill, 1971 p. 242

123. Ibid.

124. Ibid.

125. Huber, Bruno and Louise. *The Planets and their Psychological Meaning.* Hopewell, Knutsford, England. 2006. P.

126. Ibid. p. 37.

127. Op. Cit. Demot, Maureen. Appendix I

128. Op. Cit. Neuman. P. 20

129. Ibid.

130. Op. Cit. Neuman. Plate 35.

131. Op. Cit. p. 279

132. Ibid.

133. Ibid.

134. Ibid.

135. Op. Cit. Ulanov . p. 252

136. Ibid.

137. Ibid. 253

138. Op. Cit. Hall, James A. *The Jungian Experience.* P. 36

139. Op. Cit. Hall. *The Jungian Experience.* P. 81

140. Op. Cit. Huber. *The Planets.* p.34

141. Op. Cit. Hubers. *The Planets.* p. 34.

142. Ibid.

143. Freud, Anna. *The Ego and Mechanisms of Defense.* Hogarth Press, LTD. Richmond, VA. 1972. P. 5.

144. Op. Cit. Jung, C. G. *Aion.* P. 14

145. Sanford, John B. *Invisible Parters* 1980

146. Op. Cit. Hall. *The Jungian Experience.* P. 36.

147. VonFranz, Marie-Louise. *Man and His Symbols.* Aldus Books Ltd. London. 1964

148. Op. Cit. *The Cosmic Egg Timer.* P. 69

149. Jung, Emma. *Animus and Anima.* Spring Publications. Dallas Texas. 1981 pp.28-29

150. Berry, Patricia. *Echo's Subtle Body.* Spring Publications. Putnam, Conn. USA. Pp 83-85

151. Op. Cit. Jung, Emma. *Animus and Anima.* P. 34

152. Ibid.

153. Chartet, F. X. *Spiritualism Foundations of C. G. Jung's Psychology,* State University of New York. Albany, NY. 1993 P. 297.

154. Botkin, Allan, *Induced After Death Communication* Hampton Road Publishing. Charlottesville, VA. Pps.145-146

155. Cayce, Edgar ARE. Blog. Dreams About the Deceased. 2/4/2010

156. Op. Cit. Huber. *Moon Node Astrology* p. 114.

157. Op.Cit. Hopewell. *The Living Birth Chart.* P. 9.

158. Parfitt,Will. *Psychosynthesis the Elements and Beyond* PS Avalon publishers; Glastonbury, England. 2006. pps. 220-221

159. Hall. Op. Cit. p 120

160. Hillman, James. *The Force of Character.* The NY Times Company. 1999

161. Op. Cit. Hall. *Jungian Dream Experience.* P. 121

162. Op. Cit. Jung, C. G. *Aion*. P. 260

163. Langs, Robert. *Decoding Your Dreams* Ballantine Books, New York. 1988. P. 177

164. Op. Cit. Hall. *The Jungian Experience*. p. 31.

165. Jung, C. G. *Psychological Types*. Bollengen Foundation. Princeton, N.J. 1923

166. Op. Cit. Hall *Jungian Dream Interpretation*. P. 28

167. Op.Cit. Hubers. *Moon Node Astrology*

168. Op. Cit. Hall. *Jungian Dream Interpretation*. P. 31

169. Hall, James A. *Jungian Dream Interpretation*. Op.cit. P. 13-14

170a. Parfitt, Will. *Psychosynthesis the Elements and Beyond* PS Avalon; Glastonbury, England. 2006, Diagram 1

170b. Parfitt,Will, Op. Cit. p. 220

171. Ibid, p. 29 and 221

172. Parfitt, Will. Op. cit. p. 220.

173. Ibid. p. 217

174. Botkin, Allan. *Induced After Death Communication* Hampton Road Publishing. Charlottesville, VA

175. Parfitt,Will. *Psychosynthesis the Elements and Beyond* PS Avalon; Glastonbury, England. 2006.p. 219

176 VA Center for Stress Recovery Website. www.ptsd.va.gov Nightmares and PTSD.

Selected Publications on Astrological Psychology

The Cosmic Egg Timer by Joyce Hopewell & Richard Llewellyn
The best introduction to astrological psychology.

The Living Birth Chart by Joyce Hopewell
Aims to provide insight into the full power of the Huber Method
and give a feel for its practical use.

The Astrological Houses by Bruno & Louise Huber
The psychological significance of the houses.

Astrological Psychosynthesis by Bruno Huber
Bruno Huber's introduction to this holistic approach to astrology
and Assagioli's psychosynthesis. Focus on intelligence, integration,
relationships.

The Planets and their Psychological Meaning by B&L Huber
Shows how the positions of the planets are fundamental to
horoscope interpretation.

Aspect Pattern Astrology by B&L&M Huber
Understanding motivation through aspect patterns.

Aspect Patterns in Colour by Joyce Hopewell
All the main aspect patterns, fully indexed and illustrated in colour.

LifeClock by B&L Huber
The horoscope is seen as a clock for the person's lifetime, with the
Age Point indicating their age as the 'time' on the clock.

Using Age Progression by Joyce Hopewell
Practical use of Age Progression and the Life Clock.

Moon Node Astrology by B&L Huber
Psychology of the Moon's Nodes and the Moon Node Chart, giving
insight into the shadow personality and reincarnation.

Transformation: Astrology as a Spiritual Path by B&L Huber
Processes of transformation and personal/spiritual growth as natural
stages in human development, related to astrological chart.

CPSIA information can be obtained at www.ICGtesting.com
Printed in the USA
LVOW13s1046180614

390598LV00001B/66/P